Always Playing

NIGEL KENNEDY

Always Playing

WEIDENFELD AND NICOLSON · LONDON

First published in 1991 by
George Weidenfeld & Nicolson Ltd
91 Clapham High Street, London SW4 7TA

British Library Cataloguing in Publication Data applied for

ISBN 0 297 81209 2

Printed in Great Britain by
Butler & Tanner Ltd, Frome and London

Contents

Illustrations

This book is for my friends, both in the audiences and my private life, who've helped to make my career so exciting.

Nigel Kennedy

Foreword

I am really the last person qualified to write these pages – it took me months even to decide to work with him as his manager, let alone write a foreword to his book. There are classical maestros, celebrated pop stars, cultural commentators, family, friends – all of whom have known Nigel Kennedy longer than myself: a veritable army of admirers more than ready to sing the praises of this extraordinarily gifted young man. For my part, I've known him less than three years and was openly unsure about him for quite a long time. He is difficult to figure out. On the one hand he is a fashionable and fiercely independent man actively defying the establishment, looking and sounding like someone you hope your daughter wouldn't bring home to meet you. Then you witness ultra-conventional masters within the classical sphere openly enjoying both him and his performances. Quite simply, you either love or hate Nigel – it is extremely hard to dismiss him.

I have, however, known him a little longer than many of you who might have encountered him first through the release of Vivaldi's *Four Seasons*. Since planning that together, we've talked virtually every day. I've shared his fears, ambitions, triumphs: he has become an integral part of my life and yet, strangely, I've learned more about him from this book than from all the sustained personal contact. His clothes, his manners, passions are exactly the same in both public and private – and yet back there behind the public persona there is a man so private, so marked from previous experiences that you're unlikely ever to know that side of him exists: until, that is, you read this book. The only way these ribbons of emotion have previously been shared is through his performances. That is why when a piece demands joy or sadness, Nigel always manages to produce such full measures. His childhood was anything but normal and, as you will read, he shut his feelings away to the point where frustrated teachers considered he had all but hibernated emotionally. Fortunately for us, from the age of seven he was trained to channel what he felt into his performing. He takes composers' works and isolates their sentiments before stalking the dark library of his own experiences to create a match so powerful you cannot help but respond to the performance. It may not be at some traditionally controlled and rigid tempo, but it will certainly be expressing both the composer's and performer's feelings. After all, if you feel on top of the world, that emotion governs the expression. It is the same with melancholy, and for Nigel the obsession is to successfully pass that sentiment over to the listener. Reading this manuscript has completely changed much of my (and I suspect many others') thinking about the man. Until now the inevitable critics grinding on about him changing his 'image' to sell more records have been quite simply an irritant. I've neither seen nor recommended any changes since the pre-Vivaldi months when we joined forces. (How things evolved before that hadn't really concerned me.) Now, however, since reading his book so much more makes sense: the nestling up to differing musical worlds in the hope of finding a secure home; the search to belong somewhere, to be liked, and the estrangement from normal home life at so young an age. Naturally I'd known some fragments from the past, but never has he spoken at length, allowed the pieces of the jigsaw to be placed together to reveal his turbulent journey to this point. It's as though he's been awaiting sufficient courage to truly be himself.

He's not an easy man, with veritable oceans separating the topics he cares for and those he finds boring. His is a total commitment which drives him day and night to improve himself and the musical climate. I have been fortunate to work alongside a substantial list of international public figures, and yet when I come to review Nigel I would not place him high in a list of those driven by personal ambition. His drive and energy are a match for any of them and, indeed, his ability to nourish stardom through his media work makes him a perfect specimen. And yet occasional tell-tale remarks sharply remind you that what he is engaged in is rather more a crusade. His utter uninterest, for instance, in the possessions and paraphernalia of being a star is offset by almost obsessive principles on other topics. He might not thank me for mentioning it, but last year he was for the first time in his life preparing to buy a house. In a matter of three weeks he'd performed in London, San Francisco and New Zealand, and had sustained media blitzes in Australia and the Far East. With that amount of pressure and the seduction and promise of owning his first home when he returned, he still felt he had to make a stance over something he felt was wrong. An issue in England which affected his ability to buy the house remained unresolved and he phoned me from his Tokyo hotel and declared we should stick to our guns even if the house had to go. He is that kind of man. He exhibits extraordinary conviction over things he believes in, and nothing will shake him from that line of thought. He sees music as having been placed in a straitjacket, and works furiously in any way he can to help release it. How he achieves this, totally disrupting the classical establishment yet somehow still functioning as part of it, is beyond us all: he is unique. It's as though his massive energy is focused on ambitions for the music rather than for himself.

I am not a soccer man, but since Nigel became part of my life my local team has been vaguely adopted for lighthearted comparisons to his beloved Aston Villa. I encourage every non-soccer enthusiast who has read Nigel's earlier chapters to read 'Long-Gone Fathers'. Not only is it a vivid account of a growing love affair between small boy and famous club, but somehow he also manages to show you another side: how it's a lifetime's subscription to something stable, to traditions, security, a group. It makes total sense of so many Kennedy remarks and actions, and has actually changed my understanding of both his commitment to the game and indeed my perception of the sport in general. He has that easy-going way of communicating, which hundreds of thousands of fresh converts to the classical world have similarly enjoyed. Somehow, without any airs or graces, he is able to make you feel interested in the things he loves. Whether his club goes up or down in the league table has absolutely nothing to do with my world, and yet I find myself checking scores on Ceefax! His infectious spirit draws you towards his horizon. Many of the fan letters that come in show young and old alike almost surprised they have got into classical music. One irony is that he will never judge music competitions, nor lecture or preach upon the subject. His world does not embrace dictating anything to others, only sharing. He is a lover, not a teacher, of music.

The general image of a classical soloist is of someone rather detached from real life, cold, even aloof, who drifts on and off a concert platform bowing a lot in between exhibitions of skill. You don't ever get a sense they would like to remain on stage after the piece, maybe even play more. For certain there is a black, chauffeur-driven Citroën waiting outside the stage door ready to whisk the master away to wherever classicists go after successful concerts. With Nigel you can't get him off stage, and when finally he leaves his delighted audiences he promptly settles down to spend the next hour or so signing autographs and talking to them. He genuinely loves what he does.

Perhaps one of the more extreme examples of this took place not long ago when we were all shut away in a West London studio recording the extraordinary film of the Brahms Concerto. These big, barn-like rooms are not exactly glamorous, or even comfortable, and the work is exhausting. Much of the filming with the orchestra had taken place a day or two before, and so the focus of attention was upon Nigel – standing alone in front of three massive projection screens. The hours went quite smoothly. Successions of visiting executives wandered in and out of the dark warehouse setting, teas and sandwiches were laid out on a trestle table and the time rolled by. The Brahms Concerto is considered extremely difficult to play and a critic of the time actually suggested it had been composed 'against' a violin rather than 'for' one. So you can imagine that playing it without conductor or musicians in attendance is a serious test – added to which, it was being recorded on film rather than video, necessitating constant stops to change the film magazines. One way or another, not an environment you'd expect a classical soloist to put up with for long. Nigel, needless to say, was fascinated by the lighting and projected imagery supporting the moods he was creating. Quite late into the night the director, myself and the two-man camera crew were grouped around Nigel in the blackness: he had been playing Brahms virtually continuously for ten hours without any protest. We were working on a slow portion with Nigel lit by a single overhead spotlight. The loudspeakers filled the dark with the London Philharmonic, and Nigel ventured off again into this section of the concerto. That astonishing, faraway look returned to his face immediately and we stood quietly while the cameras rolled. After a while we realised the situation was changing and Nigel's face was registering more and more emotion. As the music finished the room went silent and he and the four of us just stood there, unsure who should say what first: he was so moved by the music he'd been playing for the last ten hours that tears had welled up in his eyes. After an awkward moment, there was a bit of hugging and appreciation and they reloaded the cameras again. He made a single remark to me, almost apologetically, to the effect that he couldn't help it, for without an orchestra over his shoulder to worry about, he had got lost in the music. It is those quite unguarded moments that make being close to Nigel so special: they place show-business in some other place and his music into your soul. That moment was for no one's benefit, and yet we were all affected by his magic. He has the courage to expose his feelings in every performance he gives.

Having read this book, the private battles he has waged to reach this point become all too clear. It would not seem to be a life he would wish to relive and yet it is certainly those struggles, those pains, which have created this extraordinary talent.

John Stanley
April 1991

Always Playing

Preface

I've never written a book before, but it feels as if almost every week some celebrated would-be writer wanders onto a television chat show trying hard to look cool, pretending they always walk across one-sided rooms, their face straining to remember what they or someone else has put in their book. Personally, I read quite a lot – it's a great escape, particularly with so much travelling, and I've got to admit it is intriguing to take a peep into other folks' lives. The problem though is that it's really hard to know exactly how much of it to believe. (I mean, if you had to write a book, would you really sit down and blow a peaceful life by owning up to stuff you were pretty sure you'd got away with over the years?) I guess the scent of a big cheque for various reasons can drive us to do these things, but what you write can change people's lives and relationships for ever. From what I can gather, the general trick appears to be to bore the reader to death with all the routine 'I was born in . . .', give them a handful of spicy bits and then thereafter to appear in bookshops only at signing sessions.

Over this last year quite a lot of publishers have tried to persuade me to write something. Sometimes they wanted music guides, a few were after 'a year in my life', and loads wanted a straight biography-type book. However, I have ended up sitting at this round table, tucked in the corner about to try and write. The reason? The cash certainly helps but, also, this particular invitation left it to me how I filled the pages instead of telling me what to do. Hopefully I'll be able to get my own views down on paper for you and I won't have to write bullshit – I've never had much patience with that stuff. One great thing I've already discovered – a lawyer checks it before you see it!

– CHAPTER 1 –

Volcanic Regions

Childhood is a bit tricky to get into, and I'm sure very few people really want to know about it anyway: it just happens to be where you are supposed to start a book. Anyone who might have seen a BBC television documentary about me called *Coming Along Nicely* will know it wasn't a time of sweetness and light for me, but it would be pointless to start trying to rake over such old coals just to fill pages: that fire went out a long time ago. A mixture of circumstances and musical potential fused to create a time of much unhappiness and isolation for me, of anger and of sacrifice. It was tough then but, looking back now, it becomes clear that out of all that darkness came learning experiences which I have only in my thirties come to appreciate.

Over these last few months, thinking about what I should say, I decided I would still like to go on about those early days – but not to tell you where my Mum was born or why my Dad left before I popped up. No, that's all biographical shit and I'm not ready for that yet. What I'd really like is to try and explain how I felt during those times – because, after all, I'm going to try and make it my book. Being just a 'small person' doesn't stop you forming opinions. It only means you have to sit on your fears and emotions until you grow enough for folk to listen to you. Childhood for me was a long wait for someone to listen, for an audience. Thanks to music I now have plenty of such opportunities, including it seems a book! It's all a far cry from the Regency townhouse in a Brighton square – which wasn't as grand as some social categorists might think!

My father left some months before I was born and it was a while before Mum actually discovered I was in her belly. Because the family had split up, Mum and Granny rented the top two floors to this extremely British period house complete with an ornate balcony and well-proportioned rooms. Actually, we paid our rent to the dentist who used downstairs as his place of torture: each evening he would lock up and wander off to his home leaving us to feel like we really owned the whole building. It was a great place, not exactly over-furnished or anything like that, but really a proper home in one of those very English squares you'd see featured in the old black and white films – you know, with an incredibly young-looking Trevor Howard walking around in crisp sunlight with all the neighbours saying, 'Good morning, Mr Frobisher.' There's something very special about the feeling of living by the sea: the freshness of the air, an extra brightness to the skies, the space of that horizon, that smell of the seaside. I suppose I was very lucky, but you don't think that at the time: I was simply content.

One of the main routines of family life I had to get used to was both my Mum and Granny taking on a lot of piano teaching. With my father gone this relatively low income was essential, but one inevitable consequence was that I used to get left on my own a great deal – not literally, but placed in silent suspension while someone or other struggled to make an impression on maybe a piece of Chopin. Sometimes I'd be alone on one floor while a lesson was taking place on another one. Quite often I would simply sit silently under the piano during the session. As you can imagine, it was all okay, but you couldn't get going with any sort of serious games while all that was going on. The music itself kind of pervaded my brain and my consciousness would just go with it.

Once in a while there would be the odd surprise. One lady I think must have taken pity on the little lump under the piano because she brought this huge cream-and-red-painted garage for me as a present. I didn't know then, but learned later that her gardener had built it for me: it's funny, I clearly remember our telephone number was written on the front of that building. It was brilliant because I was seriously into Dinky cars anyway – in fact, models of anything provided I didn't have to make them myself. I recall there was a set of battleships which I would lay command to across a perilous sheet of blue plastic sea, and then there were trains. A lot later I got electric ones. In fact, come to think of it, even those electric racing cars, but it was my first train that I remember most clearly. It was really tiny, about the size of those minute German ones nowadays, but this one didn't have any mechanical parts at all. It was mostly silver and there were rails to connect together as well as a few carriages. I've heard my mother say that she had once left me carefully setting pieces of the rails together on our dining room table while she went off to teach, only to find that when she eventually returned I was still engrossed in the same game. The truth was there was never any hurry, and good games took you far away across blue plastic oceans or racing over veneered landscapes to somewhere else. Besides, there was nothing else to do.

Being alone really teaches you to use your imagination. I wasn't into soldiers and things like that, but there was always a problem augmenting the train game with bodies. I suppose I was very much like many other small boys because for years I dreamed of one day becoming a train driver – not on some silent electric or diesel job, but the real thing with all that romantic smoke and power. You could feel its energy, even when it was just my silver engine throbbing its way towards the kitchen end of the table: if you got your eyes down level with the polished surface it seemed to streak by, the obedient coaches all perfectly reflected in the wood. I was definitely smitten by this most traditional of kids' fantasies, though my habit of seconding house flies as engine drivers was maybe less conventional. In fact, to be perfectly honest – which you are supposed to be in these books – that wasn't the whole story because I used to detach their wings and all but two of their legs in order that they would fit in the tiny engine cab. Nobody ever said little boys were nice!

There were never many other children to play with, except for the three daughters of my Mum's best friends who lived very close by. I used to play with one called Mary quite a lot of the time. I realise teaching must have messed with any real social routine, but I think my Mum might have been a bit sensitive about us being a one-parent family (which wasn't something much talked about in those days). Generally we seemed to keep ourselves pretty much to ourselves.

My first school was a bit of a shock to the system – you don't get any kind of warning, do you? You get through another sleepy Sunday, roast potatoes, gravy, bathtime and then, suddenly, Monday isn't normal; in fact, life isn't normal ever again. Overnight your world fills with grownups who aren't family and other kids who aren't very nice. My first encounter was at a Montessori school in Brighton called The Fold which had about fifty pupils. It was okay, I guess – not home, but interesting. If you're an only kid and you've spent quite a lot of your time on your own the appearance of dozens of kids all at one go, plus strange new house rules, is quite a shock. All I could do was systematically work it all through, trying to discover what was allowed and what wasn't, what's good news, what's bad. I remember one time wanting to try breaking a bottle. Nothing dramatic, except I smashed it over another pupil's head. I didn't mean to hurt anyone, I just wanted to try it, to see what happened. After all, it was only what I saw in the comics every week. No one was very happy with me about that, and I remember being sent to stand in the corner and later instructed to trace a porcupine as punishment. In fact I remember being on the same porcupine three weeks later because I decided to take the instruction literally and trace absolutely every spine! God knows what that teaches you about life as a grownup; maybe the teachers learned something.

I don't want to give the impression that all Mum ever did was give her attention to her pupils. She looked after me great and very early on I'd started to hit a few piano notes myself, and as I was showing interest, Mum started teaching me for fifteen minutes each morning before I went off to school. I used to have my breakfast of things like fingers of toast, which I'd hold in one hand while doing one-handed practice: it seemed the natural thing to do in our household, and a year or two later she found someone local to begin to teach me violin. There was of course also the fact that my father was a cellist (in first the Liverpool Philharmonic orchestra and then the Royal Philharmonic), and my grandfather and Granny also played cello and piano, respectively. I suppose it was really Mum's efforts which started me off on the musical journey – thanks, Mum! I think the general impression I gave to both my first school teachers and home was that I was always daydreaming – while outwardly the small body sat quietly, alone, trying not to make a nuisance of itself.

Actually, during all those early years up until I went to the Yehudi Menuhin School, at the age of seven, there was at least always Bertie: he was almost everything I wanted to be – including dark-haired (I was very blond at that time). In our private world he would always sneak off and do all the things I'd have loved to have done if I only had the courage. Naturally we talked about them in private, but that was the extent of it. Only twice did I ever come out in the open and blame dodgy deeds on him: one of them being the bottle incident at The Fold. It was really careless using Bertie's name like that, blaming him as I did, because it brought his very existence out into the open, well, at least to my Mum. He was quite simply the half of me not content just to sit under the piano and wait until the end of someone's lesson before doing things. He might have been imaginary but he was incredibly real to me: in fact, he was perhaps the first one to really listen to how I was feeling. It's strange – when you're small, adults jam your head with their opinions and you in turn dream of growing up, of people listening to your ideas, your thoughts. And yet, when you finally get there most people are so involved with their own personal set of worries you actually look back on that childhood period as being preferable. I guess something like 80 per cent of what I was formally taught at my schools, particularly at the Menuhin, I reacted to badly, but that reaction led me to trying my own alternatives and it is always such a buzz when you see your thinking work out. Bertie shared those kind of views. He actually got his name from my Mum, who had used it in some derogatory way and I thought, okay, so he's a bit of a rebel, that's cool. So there I was, living with Mum and Granny – in a great home, an only child and pretty much spoilt, a musical family backcloth, and just too much time alone. Long periods which kept launching me into my own imaginary world. Time to detach, to think.

I remember there was this window – high in the wall of my own room. It was actually an attic room, but the exciting thing I discovered was that if I stood on the end of the bed I was able to climb up onto a sort of window shelf and, with care, could look not just across Brighton but right out to sea. It was a view which held endless fascination: I could watch the constantly changing colours and moods of the open sea; the ease with which it constantly changed in character – the natural way we all accept it as angry and dangerous, and then change to worship its warmth and calmness. Quite often there would be a boat way out there, just a tiny spot. Over the hours I would climb up and down charting its slow progress until it finally slipped out of sight.

I suppose my moods too swung through a wide range of emotions: the conflict of family comfort and much attention was contrasted with getting used to boredom and being alone. It was, I think, an instinctive effort to combat the monotony of being on my own that made me sometimes become quite angry. I remember I used to spend long periods of the time tossing a coin in competition with God and making sure that I won. If I was angry with Him I used to punch at the air itself with my bare fists and, if I felt desperate sometimes, because He was meant to look down from above, I'd get up on a hardback chair, take a flying jump and whack my fists into the air so I could hit Him. It sounds pretty neurotic, but at the time I would have been about four or five and God was up there somewhere. In fact my Granny, who was a regular Church of

England sort, had always contended that she should have been a Roman Catholic and every now and then would launch forth with some kind of sermon about God being everywhere. I just took her at her word – after all, grownups are meant to be reliable, aren't they?

The chain of events which followed those first years still affects me: it was to prove both the most traumatic and maybe influential in my life. There were decisions – each considered, each in itself quite understandable, but when concentrated together they cast a darkness so dense that my spirit as a seven-year-old felt like it was wrenched into two. The half which was the child, bouncing uninhibited towards adolescence, being suspended as though on a life-support system – hoping, waiting for some more favourable moment in time to try and resume living. The other half, the survivor, that brand of determination which pulls one through traumas, rose like some phoenix from the ashes. In a matter of weeks I simultaneously developed the grit and armour of a warrior and postponed childhood. In the rush of the following months I was left with only music as a constant. It was to become my world and to fill my mind and days. It even proved to be an acceptable language to exhibit the sweep of emotions that I felt. No longer was there need to punch the air in anger or endlessly stare at lazy summer seas, for there was always new music to discover, offering that same emotional outlet. (One or two critics felt my recent recording of Vivaldi's *Four Seasons* involved passages played too fast or too slow, but if you face a score describing the brittle chill of winter and you have spent all your years fiercely focusing your feelings as well as your technical skills, then you naturally try and evoke the mood it gives you.)

This sequence of events, this upheaval which so completely changed everything was, I suppose, in part born out of my own musical development. Though not in itself a major event, the first winds of change started to blow when the dentist decided to sell up and go: the balcony I played on, the square, the tricycle rides along the beach, everything I knew had to be replaced by a small terraced house in Hove – close by the Brighton and Hove Albion football ground.

Mum, who had been doing a pretty good job on me at the piano, then decided that I was ready for something rather more challenging. Amongst the ideas she had was that I might join the then virtually new Yehudi Menuhin music school, which had just moved into fresh premises in Stoke d'Abernon. She'd already got me both a place and scholarship at Arundel School near Brighton, and so there wasn't huge pressure to earn a place elsewhere. I auditioned at the tender age of six, when the School was still in Kensington or somewhere like that; all I can really remember was that the room had the vibe of a second-grade Victorian hotel. I was too young to remember very much, but it was a really great day overall. A trip to London was quite something. We travelled up by train, which was in itself pretty exciting and then, after the audition, we went on to the zoo: it was brilliant. I can't remember exactly what I played, although it was probably something like Thomas Arne. Certainly, the main test was on the piano because I remember playing for the four of them. There was Yehudi Menuhin of course, Marcel Gazzelle (a piano teacher who played on all those great teenage Menuhin records), Peter Norris (another important teacher) and Robert Masters (who was the first violinist in Menuhin's own chamber orchestra and, I think, was also the School's musical director at that time). Once I'd done my stuff on both piano and fiddle, they took me through to another room where I was given musical tests: a bloke played me five notes and asked me to identify them. And then there were others – like playing so many notes and asking me to invent another series to follow on. Stuff like that, which I found fairly easy, and I think it was these tests that probably got me into the School for the following year: my piano playing aside, I certainly wasn't a great fiddler.

It was a quite expensive establishment but Menuhin had asked Mum if there were any financial problems. Mum admitted there were, so he explained he would deal with that. Unfortunately nothing happened and I think it was only a month or so before I was meant to start that the issue was addressed. The trouble was that the man had just so much to do, what with both the running of the School and all his performance work, that towards the deadline my Mum was saying things like 'Does he have a place there? How is it being paid for?' That kind of thing – which must have been worrying for her, as she had by then turned down the other opportunity. In the end I think Menuhin 'invented' a scholarship in memory of his parents, and he granted it to me. That's what made it possible. I was to start in the autumn term.

At almost exactly the same time, my Mum and a gentleman called Duncan were getting pretty serious. Suddenly, with my shift to a boarding school, Mum decided to move from our still new home up to Solihull to be with Duncan: in fact, they were soon married. So I inherited a new Dad and a step-sister, Joanna, who was three years older than me. Three years later my half-sister Elizabeth was born. I call her Purbur, I don't know why. She's very practical and responsible – exactly the opposite of me! In that one sweep of events I met an utterly alien boarding school environment, lost for ever what had previously been defined as home, and witnessed Mum quite naturally become rather more immersed in Duncan's world in Birmingham. Hard as I tried to rejoin this Mark II version of our family, events kept me from that new experience. To me it felt like a rough beginning for what proved to be the youngest boy in the school, and I did a pretty good job of receding into my shell. In fact, the shock was so great that even Bertie disappeared – never to show up again.

The Yehudi Menuhin School had only been open, I think, a couple of years. So, although it was meant to be for children from seven to sixteen, we were all in fact pretty young. Obviously sudden immersion in the life of a boarder is a surprise, particularly if you've previously been spoilt as an only child. The small trophies of home which I brought with me became much more important than they ever had been back in Brighton. In particular there were two koala bears and a stuffed platypus which used to stay tucked up in my dormitory bed. I think they were from Australia – from my Dad, who actually visited me twice: once really to check me out when I was born, and then again when I was five or six. The soft toys must have travelled over with him the first time – it was a train set on the second. Anyway, I would go up to the dormitory at night and there they would be – waiting, a little bit of home from home. Only home of course was no longer there. That first couple of years was really dreadful. The days before returning to school you could feel the dread welling up inside. The school clothes would start appearing in piles, the hours would tick away while apprehension grew as to whether I'd be in favour with the kids that term. I'd watch out of the window as the children returned to their Birmingham school and would long to be one of them. The actual day of departure was terrible. There would be the long drive back with us all subdued and uneasy. Mum was always making promises in an attempt to carry the day: if I really didn't like it I could leave the next term. Other times she suggested she might come and work at the School. They became ritual remarks, a kind of game of charades while piecemeal I was actually getting through school. Mum reminded me recently, when we talked about this time, that she once apologised for the long and boring journey. Apparently, I answered that it didn't matter at all because I knew I'd have to get used to being bored – for when I grew up.

Once we'd arrived, as soon as possible after the actual goodbyes, I'd venture into the television room and hide my pain in the half-light of something like *Danger Man* or *The Avengers*. After a little while and much swapping of newly acquired sweets, storytelling of the holidays would break out, and we remained okay until the harsh realities of our surroundings reappeared in the dormitory.

The actual school terms seemed to stretch on forever. The weekends however were brilliant because there was not only free time but also plenty of companionship – something I was learning to relish. I recall at one time harbouring a serious crush on a strawberry blonde called Rosemary, who was around my age but somehow seemed a lot older. For months I thought the world of her, but I was much too busy joking around to do anything constructive about it. Then, just one time, I remember she was up in a balcony some place and I was on the lawn down below. I was running towards her saying, 'I love you, Rosie. I love you,' like in a movie, but she just looked down and said, 'If you really meant it, then maybe we'd have something to talk about.' I just didn't know what to do. Actually, thinking about it, there was another girl that had a whole bunch of us fascinated. Obviously, unlike a normal school, we were there because our families and former music teachers considered each of us to be the best. Curiously, talent and determination were almost pre-assumed – and so it was thought around the corridors that this particular girl, whom we considered pretty rough musically, was in fact a teacher's spy planted in our very midst. There again, maybe it was an experiment to see if a particularly untalented kid could be made to learn music!

Unlike the charms of weekends, the weekdays were a real struggle and I know there was a good deal of teacher frustration over my introverted ways. Without boring you, maybe the easiest way to establish that picture would be through the eyes of my then headmaster, Anthony Brackenbury. His school reports first remarked: 'The "Benjamin" of our household: the youngest and everybody's favourite. We try not to spoil him, but it's a hard job.'

Then followed, 'He is something of a dormouse, and much of the time seems to be hibernating. I suppose this is another way of describing the "latency" period when adults have to call on their reserves of patience.' Which led to, 'There have been some signs this term that he is on the move, but we shall have to be patient while this group of small boys works through the barbarian stage of comics, of silly words, of ganging up. What about positive comments? By sheer perseverance he has learned to skip, and his end-of-term acting had a new vitality.'

Then, 'Does the road wind uphill all the way? I can imagine Nigel wondering this as he plods on. Maybe it does, but at least he has the satisfaction of knowing that each term he is further on, higher up, and I hope enjoying a better view.'

In the summer of '67 he observed, 'I have been delighted to see him exert himself bravely at non-babyish things – swimming for example, tennis and jumping. Instead of just thumping his chest and shouting "Olé" and imagining the rest, he now begins to see that he can really grow up and do things too. Hooray.'

By the end of '69 he was remarking, 'He is at a transitional stage and in fits and starts wants to begin growing up and to leave the small boy behind.'

In the autumn it had become, 'Nigel is on the uneasy threshold of growing up; at one moment childish and irresponsible, at another serious and committed. In the midst of the muddle there are signs of very promising development.' Then followed, 'His comfortable appearance conceals a good deal of volcanic matter, but even after seven years he remains strangely uncommunicative. I think he finds it almost impossible to communicate himself with his own volcanic regions ... but I would like him to be more in touch in case of need.'

By the winter of '72 he was saying, 'Some diffidence and anxiety which we have seen in the past seems to be disappearing. Certainly he holds his own in A class and more than holds his own as a musician. His strong individual personality is beginning to emerge.'

Obviously that doesn't trace the musical studies, just the headmaster's own general comments, but concealed behind that parade of opinions I was trying to form some of my own. It was a brilliant education, but once I'd got over the shock of losing home, of Mum remarrying, the advent of a step-sister and, eventually, a half-sister – plus not really being able to regroup with this new family in its surroundings – I put all my thoughts into the music. I guess I challenged the education right from the start, but my own emotional bruising prevented it coming to the surface for the first couple of years. However, from about the age of ten I learned to embrace about 20 per cent of the advice given and to discard the other 80 per cent.

For the first years I did everything I was told and really didn't make any progress at all and, although this wasn't something I could make a conscious evaluation of, by the time I was eleven or twelve, I started doing things for myself. If the teacher would say play it like that, I'd play it like that. Yes, play it like that in the day and then do it entirely differently, my way, at night in front of some small audience. What was really exciting was that communicating my musical feelings rather than the School's appeared to please everyone, including me. I remember there was this real disciplinarian of a lady teacher who used to insist that you've got to wear the jacket, you've got to wear the tie before you could perform. She used to stand backstage to check the tie was straight and the jacket on, and then she'd send us through the door onto stage. I used to hate that and felt really uncomfortable, so after I while I would wait until she'd closed the door again and put my violin down, take off my jacket, loosen the tie and then get stuck into playing. The audience thought this was a riot, but I felt free to play. At the end I'd receive the applause and then put the jacket back on, straighten up the tie and walk back through the door past her. I think she was a bit suspicious that I enjoyed so much clapping from the crowd before I started playing, but it was about five or six concerts before she discovered. Of course, once I was on stage she couldn't do much about it, as I was with people who understood – the audience.

As if the alienation from school life wasn't enough, there was this BBC television crew who kind of adopted me at the age of fourteen and, over the next few years, focused much personal attention on me – both at Menuhin and, subsequently, at the Juilliard School in New York. One way or another, hard as I tried to hide out, it wasn't the way it was meant to be.

I really didn't want to turn this book into a long, detailed account of my past. What I did set out to try and do, though, was to give you a picture of the major events which coloured my schooldays in the hope it would help to illustrate how I came to choose to rely on my own opinions and feelings rather than those from more conventional quarters – such as family or school. Certainly losing home life and not getting recoupled to its new incarnation made me self-reliant and perhaps less trusting. Also, the rather unreal nature of the Menuhin School placed me initially in a void – which, as I filled it with my own visions, heightened the strength of my emerging private convictions. With no conventional timetable, a seven- or eight-year-old alone in a room for three hours to practise creates a ready hotbed for both doubts and dreams.

As we crept into the phase where the schooling felt like one long stretch of technical development, I began to see the excitement within the world of jazz. At night I would listen secretly to broadcast jazz works on a portable radio in bed. The whole vibe of great players enjoying their music flooded across the airwaves and drew a sharp contrast to the rigidity and anonymity of what I was going through at school. Through listening to this stuff, I was awake much later than all the others and thus pretty wrecked in the morning, so I used to catch up on my sleep by putting my head in my hands and dozing off. Obviously, in the academic subjects I couldn't get away with this, but in some of the music things where we were all sitting around listening to some cadence of music, I used to get a bit of a doze. I would sit next to a friend who'd nudge me when it was getting round to my turn to comment on something.

I suppose this interest in a wider spectrum of music started to turn into something a lot more serious. I managed to get one or two mates at the school to start playing jazz with me, and I gather Menuhin knew what I had been doing. He was friends with Stephane Grappelli, and I think he must have been tipped off about me because when he came to play to the School, I'd been told he might invite other players up on stage and Peter Norris (the School's music director) had actually told me to take my fiddle, just in case. Standing up there with him was absolutely 100 per cent excitement, heightened even more by the fact that I was playing such stuff within the School. Thinking back on that time, between the newly inflamed passion for creative jazz work and my already declared commitment to the Aston Villa soccer team, it might seem a miracle my classical output did not suffer. In fact I was living proof that a broad range of experiences (as opposed to specialisation) can benefit a musician because at that time my improvement was probably the fastest out of all the students at the school, making up for my lack of progress in my earlier years. Ironically, the BBC television interest also stemmed in part from jazz: Paddy Foy from the TV series *Gala Performance* had heard me playing at the School and invited me to appear in the show. I remember I'd been sent to the studio in my own car to play the slow movement from the Bruch Concerto. Backstage I'd made quite a point of wanting to be away by ten – not because I had to be back at school, but because Dizzy Gillespie was performing in London. This appeared to intrigue them, and so it all started.

At sixteen, immediately after leaving the Menuhin establishment, I flew over to the Tanglewood summer school in the United States and then into the renowned Juilliard School of Music in New York City. Not only did that move place me in a much more rigid classical teaching environment, but it also took me right to the very doorstep of the thriving New York jazz fraternity. The energy coming out of some of the clubs was wonderful, the freedom for musicians to enjoy what they were playing, to actually express themselves, was absolutely brilliant. There was real friendship between all these different players – united in their love of good music. It was like some magical society, with its own handshakes and buzz words. You can imagine how seductive that was for someone who had been largely strapped to the conventions of classical music since the time I'd learned to walk. It always makes me smile when some journalist or another decides that I have just conjured up some kind of 'Kennedy-speak', and that this has been contrived to help sell copies of my *Four Seasons*. If they had bothered to research the old broadcast tapes they would have found I have always pretty much blended in with my surroundings. You can easily spot someone who's just off a plane from the USA by the harmless use of mid-Atlantic. I started out with a very standard middle-class vocabulary, then drifted into something a little less 'plum in the mouth', which proved an easier passport to both the players in my group and the stands at Villa. If you then add three years of exposure to all breeds of musician in New York, then I guess you'll end up with something like yours truly: handshakes and all. I'd have had to be deaf and dumb, or totally insensitive, not to let some of the experiences rub off on me.

– CHAPTER 2 –

Foreign Values

I wonder if you've ever had that feeling of disappointment – the kind whereby you've been planning, say, a mega holiday somewhere very special. You've read all the books, studied movies set in that landscape, even watched the currency exchanges in the paper with a partisan eye. Everything new, clothes, luggage, all assembled – only to find nearly all of the famous movie was actually shot somewhere else, the books didn't mention your hotel's proximity to the airport, and you need most of your local currency just to buy a lager. Preconceptions are a dangerous commodity.

Having taken three years at the Menuhin School to steady from the shock of family changes, raise my courage, music and confidence, I naturally viewed with much excitement extending myself in the grownup environment of the Juilliard. Leave school, join a college and sharpen both the man and the career. Wrong. I suppose that sounds pretty arbitrary and certainly I wouldn't want to convey suggestions that the place was shit: it wasn't. But if I'm to write down how I actually feel, then it would be a pretence to suggest it was what I had anticipated. Certainly, on the face of it, it was all there – loads of talented students and teachers, great facilities and the electric ambience of New York City. What I hadn't anticipated was that the period spent there would actually move me further away from my goals. Such were the conventions that expressing yourself was even more severely frowned upon than back in England. Over the past eighteen months there have been critics who've suggested that I'm just using classical music as a ticket to notoriety, which obviously doesn't sit well when you've been immersed in nothing but music virtually from birth, and you then have writers gaining notoriety by writing about you. If these critics, who one hopes also have been focused solely on perfecting their craft since kindergarten, want to see self-promotion and ambition eclipsing the real emotions of music, visit such an American classical school: there is the stench of raw ambition, of ruthless professional people only too happy to conform to whatever is musically suitable to succeed. It must be heartbreaking for the composers – wherever dead composers sit to watch what goes on down here. All that wonderful, passionate material being homogenised to ensure everything is manicured, no new blood breaks through the standard ways. It's a miracle anyone freshly interested in classical music is tempted to venture forward while such tidy clones of conformity are being nurtured. My Elgar, Vivaldi or Brahms may or may not be the best technical recordings in the world, but they are played with a love and a passion that I don't apologise for exposing – and well over a million people in different countries have said, 'Yes, I like that one,' and bought it (over two million counting all my recordings).

Perhaps the American school attitude is cool in the closed involvement of their establishment, but these concertos were painstakingly composed in order to get the emotion the writer felt across to the audiences – and audiences to me are those who choose to leave home and spend their money on theatre seats. Mr Great Composer sweated blood to get his feelings out and centuries later, audiences make a conscious effort to try and recapture the fullness of that man's passion. Why then does the classical fraternity doggedly work at keeping these two elements so far apart? Don't misunderstand me, the Juilliard School was full of brilliant players all hungry to succeed, but it was their progress which preoccupied them and not the discovery of the music and its emotions. As an example, I worked with Dorothy DeLay, who is one of the world's great fiddle teachers, and her guidelines included the rule every student had to go up to the conductor at the end of a concert and shake his hand and say, 'What a wonderful concert,' in the hope that they got a gig out of it. Stuff like that, which was simply trying to breed professional opportunity rather than better music. Students came up and wouldn't be talking about the music. Instead they were saying, how did I get that manager? How did I get that gig? It was a lot like that. I guess things like the BBC television crew following me around must have looked like heaven to those mentalities, but the attention for me stemmed from being a six-year-old with a fire in the belly that Sir Yehudi Menuhin sensed – indeed, sponsored.

Let me give you another example: it was an awful episode, of which I was actually quite proud at the time. Stephane Grappelli was playing in town at the Carnegie Hall and, naturally, I was backstage with him before the show. Dorothy DeLay had told me not to play jazz anywhere, and then Stephane started doing one of his 'Oh, my boy, you should play . . .' speeches. I explained to him that my teacher had said I shouldn't, and he was just so disappointed. How could I insult such a great musician? And so I drank half a bottle of whisky, altered my decision and went on stage. Everyone thought it was a huge success and then, about two days later, I was having a lesson with Dottie again and she said, 'I've heard something. Do you want to tell me anything?' I said, 'No' (I'd actually forgotten about the gig by then), and she went on to announce that she knew I'd been on stage. She then proclaimed that there had been two CBS A & R classical music people there and that as a result I'd never record classical music for that label because of that one jazz appearance.

It actually took a little while for the full force of such a statement to sink in. It had in fact been one of my better nights. Then I began to think, 'Shit – is the music business really like this? Can one really be punished for playing good music, whatever form it might be?' I'm not trying to suggest like status, but can you imagine some gallery owner saying to Van Gogh, 'No, sorry, that's not an oil painting, that's a watercolour, now you've done this I'll make sure you don't ever hang in my galleries.' With those sorts of attitudes classical music doesn't deserve an industry.

I simply continued to stretch the rules as far as I could, and gradually missed more and more classes – playing extra live gigs on my own instead. At night I would be playing jazz dates and, inevitably, missing the morning classes, which caused a lot of arguments with the teachers. The trouble was that their standards of teaching in, for example, the theory of music weren't nearly as advanced as they had been at the Menuhin School. They actually had singers in the class, and it's traditionally known that singers know sod all about music! What I think really got to them was that at the end of term I would sit the examinations like everyone else and still come out with good results, without having attended the classes. That obviously didn't breed friendships, but what was I supposed to do? I know there were a lot of heated discussions as to whether to grant me the credits due from these exams – which in the end I did receive. I think they refused to accept my results and credits in the last year simply because I was barely attending the school and they felt part of getting the credits involved the discipline of turning up. There really wasn't much point in arguing over that issue.

I maintained some of my studies at the school, but I guess the old Kennedy defence mechanisms started falling into place. You simply have to follow your instincts: I know if I play a piece wrongly or mis-select repertoire the audience will give me clear signals. That detection process is a vital part of a performer, but the same process also tells me what listeners enjoy and they, at least, are never governed by traditional misconceptions. To them it's good, exciting, moving, boring or simply bad. That's great, that's the way it should be. Brahms, Beethoven – any of them would be happy to stand or fall on such judgement. Whether it happens to be classical, jazz, ecclesiastical, pop, dance – whatever, the public's taste should still remain the judge.

It's ironic, but looking back on that period I'm certain that if I'd elected to stay and live in the States I would have almost certainly given up classical performing and emerged with some kind of group.

The classical fraternity I encountered was clinically ambitious and emotionally sterile and, to me, the jazz world appeared just the opposite. However, all those tender years had engraved on me my excitement for classical music and so Sir Yehudi's passion for the European traditions rose in me like some cultural battle flag. Although I didn't stay the full course at the Juilliard, I did put in three years. However, things started to happen for me back in Britain.

One of the main sponsors for my American studies was also associated in some way with the Philharmonia Orchestra, and I gained an audition to perform at the Festival Hall with their main conductor Riccardo Muti. This was actually the performance the BBC filmed as the culmination of their long years of checking me out. That concert and the resultant exposure brought me to Menuhin's agent and quite a number of concert opportunities. (The fact that I pulled out a Villa scarf in the first tutti of the Mendelssohn – to make sure my debut was memorable! – didn't particularly endear me to Riccardo: maybe he supports Juventus or something!) That was in fact when I decided to leave the Juilliard School and return home to try and establish a career. I wanted to work, not merely become just a top-class student. In fairness to Dottie and her dire warnings about mixing the musical interests, Menuhin too had on occasion suggested that I should limit the conflict within myself. Then, once I had displayed some credible concert work at the Festival Hall, the agent started on the same topic. When two or three figures independently recommend the same course of action, only a fool wouldn't review the notion. So I found myself declaring that I intended to perform no more jazz concerts and would be concentrating on the established career. Now, of course, I look back on that triangle of advice and realise that they collectively represent the very establishment I was trying to penetrate. I did make a lot of friends in my three years in New York, and I'm sure my technique benefited from the extended attention it received. But at that moment my eagerness to communicate the music, though stimulated by the cultural contrasts, was nevertheless subdued.

London felt very strange. Since the age of seven I had been almost totally insulated from the real world by a virtually closed community of music schools. Over the years, all my decisions had been largely taken for me; my financial needs were always ensured (with a bit of help from New York street busking), and the dictate had always been, 'Be like the rest of the students.' Harbouring a kind of passive intellectual rebellion was all very well, but suddenly I was back in town without the moral support of clusters of fellow students. The classical establishment had taken their perfunctory glance at my skills and placed me on probation. It was not the time to be weak.

Once I returned, I moved in with Duncan's sister and brother-in-law, my aunt and uncle. It was another little attic room, but this time without a private view out to sea. Actually it was in one of those stunning Regency terraced houses around Regents Park, which was a wonderful place to live. Practising, though, was a bit of a problem because I always had to find places to play that were as far as possible away from my aunt's consulting rooms: she was a psychoanalyst and needed to provide the impression that there was total privacy and no one else was in the house. I'd sometimes work in the kitchen, and at other times in my uncle's study which was fairly soundproof. The most important house rule was that I always had to stop playing at ten minutes to each hour and remain silent until ten past every hour, because this was the time when her clients were coming in and out of the building and it was all a bit sensitive, as some of them didn't want to be discovered. It was a strange vibe, but at least it was a quiet house, that is when this mad youngster wasn't grinding away in the kitchen!

Naturally enough, my main concern was to practise hard and gradually develop concert confidence with the main pieces of repertoire. That discipline of working out for a few hours every morning is still maintained well over a decade later, and has been a cornerstone to getting past that comfortable point of knowing the piece and on into the much more challenging area of feeling and emphasising it. What quite often happens with classical soloists is that they set up this kind of antiseptic barrier which prevents them from being criticised because they take a 'holier than thou' sort of attitude. Kind of defying criticism and at the same time preventing themselves from having to lay their emotions open. It's a very safe way of getting through performances without too much trouble, but that's not enough for me. I've always wanted to express the emotional elements of the music because it is one of the main languages for communication. It does mean you are very exposed to the critics, but I don't worry very much about them – providing I know I've made the all-important contact with the audience itself.

The big Muti gig had gone really well and having been televised, I felt pretty good about things. Ironically, the major opportunity that this exposure brought me was an invitation to record the Mozart concertos for CBS, which appeared to suggest my playing jazz in New York hadn't caused the lifetime ban the school had foreseen. Probably at that age I could have recorded them quite well, because they weren't exactly the most mature concertos Mozart wrote, hardly the deepest, and so I would have gone in and recorded them without questioning their content as maybe I do nowadays. Unfortunately my agent said that it wasn't right for a young person to play Mozart. In fact, she started to say this directly to the record company – who simply told us to go away. One or two more things happened like that, and then I moved agent within that organisation. So as it ended up I had achieved the big Festival Hall gig and then it all fell away again to bits and pieces. Naturally I didn't have my own audience in those days, so it was very much a matter of walking into classical institutions and doing gigs completely on their terms. It was all very different from my teenage ambitions and dreams of being free to play good music – whatever type it happened to be at the time. The Muti concert was fine because it gave me a real chance to play that piece to the very best of my ability – for me half the challenge of pursuing a classical career is the process of forever trying to improve both the conditions and the playing: the very dull, standard concerts I was otherwise getting were a very long way from this philosophy. I think one of the things that kept me going was having so many young friends who were finding it incredibly hard to get work, or were having to play things they really didn't want to in order to live. This made me feel lucky – I was at least chasing the career I wanted, even if the conditions were still far from ideal.

It was around this time, when I would have been nineteen or twenty, that doubt began emerging as to whether I might not be happier simply dropping the classical side and returning to New York and the more friendly world of jazz. There were just so many foreign values and conditions attached to classical music, and all this protocol stuff with which the agents were preoccupied – career moves which were so inconsequential, a lot of time being spent on getting very little further on. There wasn't a chance for anything I was playing to break through this barrier and actually make people feel what I was feeling. I used to stay very closely in touch with my friends in New York, and every so often I would go out there, play a gig or two and spend time with them. Strangely, Dorothy DeLay proved an invaluable friend: she was very orthodox, but at least she had nothing to do with the British classical scene and, as such, was very detached. It helped me a great deal to be able to play for her and get a renewed sense of my own worth and potential. Naturally, she was keen I continued along the chosen path, even if it looked like being a cul de sac, and even if every concert opportunity was me opening with Mendelssohn followed by a performance of Bruckner, inevitably to audiences of just mature ladies.

I suppose if I try and put all this in perspective my reviews were actually among the best a British violinist had enjoyed. I think what I was detecting was an attitude in the profession that as I wasn't Israeli or Russian, I wasn't going to be taken seriously. I'd hear someone from France or somewhere else playing much worse than me and yet they got better reviews simply because they were from a cred country. Fortunately, instead of discouraging me, it made me more determined than ever that I would work and work at my playing until there simply wasn't any dispute about who was the better violinist – it just seemed to me the best way to fight prejudice. The fact that I'd been performing and developing the Elgar was helping a bit because, although an English fiddler might be a bit of a professional oddity, the critics were at least comfortable with such a domestic animal interpreting this very English music.

When I look back on that period in my life there was always something in the diary which kept the flame alive, even if the in-between periods felt eternal. The Muti was good for quite a respectable time and then I got a gig playing the Elgar, with Menuhin conducting, at the Festival Hall. That was a very, very big gig for me – in fact, the only important one I had at that time. Actually, it was a bit too big really because working with Menuhin, who was totally identified with the Elgar concerto, made it a bit of a pressure. Quite a lot of people were saying that I was the next one to step into his shoes, become the guardian of that concerto, and Sir Yehudi was getting a little upset by this. I remember him on one television show protesting it wasn't right to say such things and that he hadn't stopped playing the piece yet, basically being protective of his own territory. He became quite adamant about how things were to be done in that performance and I totally obeyed whatever he said – I was going to play it just like him. So, on the night, I spent some time focusing myself, really getting into the perfect state of mind for the piece, remembering all the directions he had given me over the years and more immediately during concert rehearsals. I felt the actual performance was really moving and that I had truly got into the spirit of the music. Oddly, this was one time in my career when the reviews proved to be valuable because they said my performance was very similar to Menuhin's, but then begged the question, was it good enough to simply be like him? After that I really stopped and thought about it all: I knew I was playing like him, but I had thought it was a great thing to do. There are a lot of players in the classical world who make a very good career out of playing like somebody else. Strangely, when I saw this criticism written down, it didn't sit well with me and I felt it wasn't good enough. This was one of the biggest discoveries I was to make, just how little of me was actually there to be witnessed. Sure I played okay, but much of my style and technique actually belonged to my stronger teachers from over the years.

It was time to tear down all those indoctrinated values. My own personality and interpretation was overshadowed by others, and I had to face a really massive reclamation process to re-establish my own individuality again. Both my personality and my playing had become very passive, which is the sort of bloke Menuhin is, and I had now to start asserting myself. He never really expresses his aggression in music. Never, and when there are aggressive bits sometimes it sounds a bit distorted because he doesn't know how to express that emotion. The way I set about redressing this influence was by returning to the composers' scores. I looked at each of their original directives – saying, 'Am I doing that?' Interestingly, there were many discrepancies between what Menuhin was doing, however brilliant, and what was actually written in the scores. I decided to go for what the composers had written, evolving my own feelings drawn from that direction. I couldn't just stop work to reappraise my style and intentions, because performing was my job, and so I had to start the process standing up there in front of audiences. With my feelings towards fans it will come as no surprise to learn that that was the perfect environment for changes, corrections – taking me back towards my own feelings. The audience would warm to those aspects which I knew were really mine and not some other teacher's, and that confirmation was all I needed to extend myself still further. One paying customer out front is worth much more than an army of professionals: he knows what he likes, what feels real to him, what is worth leaving home to see. That support was all that I needed to journey back towards individuality.

By this time my uncle and aunt had bought a flat in Fitzjohn's Avenue, with the intention of moving into it themselves. However, they said in the meantime I could rent it from them – and so I shared it with another ex-Menuhin student piano player, Kathryn Stott, and her boyfriend, Mick. It was a much healthier environment to practise in and being all musicians made it a very comfortable base for the next year or two. Until I got married to Joanna in fact, and we moved to Oxfordshire.

Joanna was a friend of Kathryn's, although she wasn't actually a musician. The Oxfordshire adventure didn't last long, and we returned to our own flat further along Fitzjohn's Avenue. Our marriage lasted six years, despite the rotten pressures of my business, and in the end we parted in a civilised way without destroying each other or our friendship.

To get back to what I was saying, the more I thought about the Elgar the more it became an obvious target for my attention. I even went to his home to study his original manuscripts – which actually proved to be virtually identical to the published editions. The countryside he lived in, those beautiful rolling hills – he was simply brilliant at transmitting what he saw, was feeling at the time, and going there was like breathing life into his score. Gradually everyone seemed to start supporting me with this concerto. I played it with James Loughran and the Halle Orchestra and the writer Michael Kennedy (no relation!) gave it a great review: suddenly I was being encouraged to put more and more of myself into it. Then I got a chance to work with the conductor Vernon Handley, who had enjoyed great success with Elgar recordings and was considered an authority on that composer. After we'd played together he was totally supportive of what I was doing with this work and encouraged me to go on doing it 'the Kennedy way'. At last I was being given an opportunity to be myself, and yet work within the magical world of great music.

It was about this time that the famous fiddle player Salvatore Accardo cancelled his appearance at the Royal Festival Hall, and suddenly I found I was replacing him and returning to that hall, to the scene of the Menuhin revelations, to perform the Elgar again – this time with Sir Charles Groves conducting. Only now I went back to do it on my terms, with a clearer idea of my own visions for the piece and a great deal more confidence. However obstinate I might have been over those years, insisting on giving my own impressions a chance, I felt sure in time it would pay off. Sir Charles, the audience, even the critics were all very flattering about the performance and Todd (that's what we all call Vernon Handley) began to talk about getting together to record.

It was also around this time that I found a great deal of inspiration from the fascinating British fiddle player Albert Sammons. He was pretty much self-taught and I think he only had something like twelve violin lessons. He ended up being the equivalent of, say, Kreisler, only he was British, didn't have a very exciting name and generally didn't aspire to great fame like some of the others. There were just two recordings of the Elgar which I loved – one was the Menuhin, and the other was a historic version made by Sammons, which was totally different and yet got completely to the heart of the work and was recorded proof that you could successfully do it on your own terms. His was more direct and less concentrated on each detail, making more of the architecture of the whole work. Menuhin's version expands every second of the work – which means it can turn into a kind of rhapsodic fifty-minute event with great moments of inspiration – whereas Sammons's is a direct view of the piece. He made it possible to understand the whole thing. It was great, and a big influence on my thinking.

Todd's ideas about recording the concerto together involved using a mid-priced EMI label. I knew there was no chance I would achieve this goal on a more prestigious full-priced version, simply because there were no significant British fiddlers on full-price: it really was that prejudicial. Maybe one or two conductors got contracted, Jacqueline du Pré had been the last artist, and then James Galway got in on his flute – but no British artist on fiddle or piano. As I

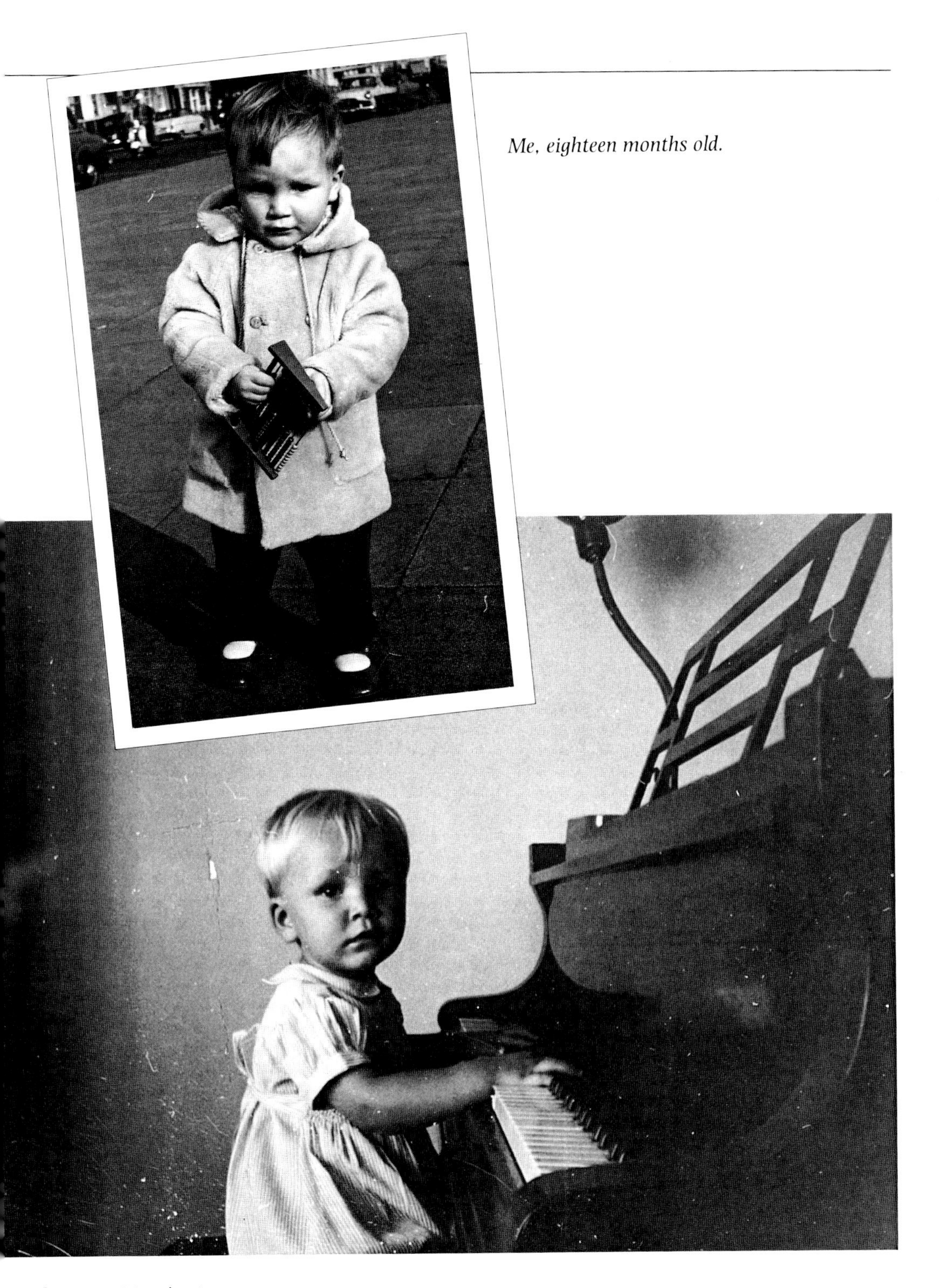

Me, eighteen months old.

Aged two, at Mum's piano.

On the balcony of our flat in Brighton.

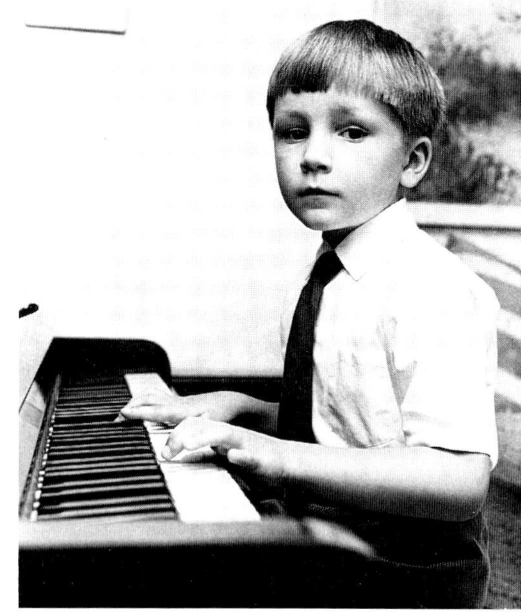

In 1964, after winning the scholarship to the Menuhin School.

n Nadia Boulanger's class at the Menuhin School – I was the youngest kid in the school, and according o the teachers I was thought to be in hibernation.

With Sir Yehudi Menuhin and Robert Masters – two great teachers.

Eight years old, on my way back to school. That's my stepfather Duncan smoking his pipe.

'he wedding photograph: Mum and Duncan in the middle, with Granny, Duncan's sisters and their usbands, and my step-sister Joanna.

YEHUDI MENUHIN SCHOOL

NAME Nigel Kennedy | SUBJECT General | DATE December 1964

The 'Benjamin' of our household: the youngest, and everybody's favourite. We try not to spoil him but it's a hard job.

Antony Brackenbury

YEHUDI MENUHIN SCHOOL

1

NAME Nigel Kennedy | SUBJECT General | DATE Spring 1967

He is still something of a dormouse and much of the time seems to be hibernating. I suppose this is another way of describing the 'latency' period when adults have to call on their reserves of patience

AHBrackenbury

YEHUDI MENUHIN SCHOOL

NAME Nigel Kennedy | SUBJECT General | DATE Winter 69

He is at a transitional stage, & in fits & starts wants to begin growing up & to leave the small fry behind. He seems to get on well with everyone, myself included, but he is not sure enough of himself in some funny way to look me square in the eye.

AHBrackenbury.

YEHUDI MENUHIN SCHOOL

NAME Nigel Kennedy | SUBJECT General | DATE Summer 71

His comfortable appearance conceals a good deal of volcanic matter but even after seven years he remains strangely uncommunicative. I think he finds it almost impossible to communicate himself with his own volcanic regions. But I would like to be more in touch in case of need.

AHBrackenbury

YEHUDI MENUHIN SCHOOL

NAME Nigel Kennedy | SUBJECT General | DATE Winter 72

Some diffidence & anxiety which we have seen in the past seems to be disappearing. Certainly he holds his own in 'A' and more than holds his own as a musician. His strongly individual personality is beginning to emerge.

AHBrackenbury

BOVE *With Stephane Grappelli. The nearest anyone got to being my idol.*

EFT *A few of my school reports from the Menuhin School.*

SATURDAY, 22 JUNE 5.30 for 6.0

MELVYN TAN NIGEL KENNEDY
Pupils of the Yehudi Menuhin School
Piano and Violin Recital

Nigel Kennedy, violin, is 17, his father a distinguished Australian 'cellist and his mother a pianist. He joined the school in 1964 as the first holder of the Menuhin Scholarship. Has played in chamber music groups at Gstaad and Windsor Festivals as well as in the USA. Hopes to continue his studies at Juilliard School in New York next year, and meantime been offered a scholarship to attend Tanglewood summer school in the USA. An enthusiast of football and jazz.

Melvyn Tan, piano, is 17. Chinese by birth, he came to the school in 1969 on the strength of a tape recording made in his home town of Singapore. Has appeared on numerous occasions both on his own and as an accompanist, and is hoping to continue his studies next year at the Royal College of Music. Enjoys ballet and is a great reader.

Tickets: £2.50, £1.75, 90p, 65p.

Separate tickets, £2.30, for supper in a basket and Charleston Cup suitable for a summer evening.

Bar.

In my last year at the Menuhin School Melvyn Tan and I played at the Charleston Festival, organised by Lady Birley who lived at the house. I remember meeting Virginia Wade that day.

said, it was very much 'foreigners are holier than us' at that time.

The actual background to my recording was full of twists of fate: the London Philharmonic Orchestra had this agreement to do a sponsored series of recordings with EMI and I later learned there was just sufficient left in the fund for the company to commission a small group album booked to be recorded in Watford Town Hall (which is often used for quite large recordings). The intended piece of Walton actually involved the use of two actors and one of them pulled out at very short notice. The then head of Music For Pleasure, Simon Foster, had been to see my Elgar concert and there had been some internal discussions about it as a future project. Given this recording crisis, Simon was rushing around with only two weeks to the date. Absolutely by chance his two recording days were free in my diary and, unbelievably, the two prior ones saw me performing the very concerto in Bournemouth, and the two subsequent days also had me doing the same piece with the Halle. I was pencilled in, but then there was the problem of trying to retrieve well over half the orchestra – who hadn't been booked for the session – plus, naturally, the funds to suddenly pay for this pretty substantial work.

Somehow it was all scraped together in time, and I turned up to record without ever rehearsing with the players. Mind you, Todd was there and he knew how I approached the music. It all went quite smoothly, although over the next few performances, away from the inevitable pressures of my very first concerto recording, I began to see more and more within the piece I wished I had incorporated.

It was sometime later when it went on to win the *Gramophone* magazine Record of the Year award, which was a real recognition that the classical world could accept individuals not conent with the status quo. Curiously, it was the very first concerto recording ever to win this award, because normally it was either a symphony or an opera or something like that which won. The British Phonographic Industry awards are a much more glitzy affair with much wider definitions embracing all forms of music. In many ways, being shortlisted for their Classical Record of the Year meant even more because it was listed alongside all these giants in the whole music scene: kind of living proof that music could be all one world. Obviously, being a cut-price record didn't put us in a very good position and no one could even remember a cheap release gaining an award in the face of the full-priced albums. Then, suddenly, absolutely a surprise, I find myself walking up to the stage under the glare of television lights to receive the Classical Record of the Year award from Sir Georg Solti, who called me Michael Kennedy. Naturally, it was a very gratifying moment for me but, strangely perhaps, the most appealing thing about that day was being on that stage, sharing the event with all other musicians from the contemporary world whom I so admired. It was as though I'd been accepted into the fraternity despite the brand of music I was representing. That moment gave me an appetite, a resolve that whatever happened in my career, I should follow my instincts, my desires to get my music accepted into wider public circles.

There was quite a lot of publicity around that event, and afterwards EMI started to discuss a proper recording contract – although, typically, they were quite reluctant about the prospect of a lowly Englishman becoming a solo star. Eventually at least a domestic contract happened and the Tchaikovsky recording started a progression of my releases.

The pattern of professional life became quite set, with regular bookings, mostly with the same parties, stretching away into future years at pre-fixed fees without any regard for what piece of music I might be into at that stage in my life or what my value might be then: I guess the assumption was that not much would change. Once a year there might be a modest fee rise, kind of like keeping pace with inflation. It gave me a very strange feeling, one that only the crazed highs and lows of show-business could provide. Having discovered at the Menuhin concert that I was turning into some kind of traditional stereotype, only to force myself back into shape and winning the top awards, I found myself, loosely speaking, as part of the establishment – reluctantly hanging on to its coattails but not really becoming either comfortable or truly accepted. Awards, recording deal, concerts, but still not that excitement, that sense of something really special with the audience. I longed for that closeness, that warmth with them, whether it was sharing the secret of lost jacket and tie or the electricity of the slow movement of Bruch. Without that bond it all became very sterile.

The record company longed to get me into proper evening dress and equally, I was sick to death of being edged towards something I never was nor wanted to become. It was unspoken, but it was sort of, 'Now you're part of our world, you must be like us if you really want to go further.' Tragically, there just weren't any options for me. No alternative routes for my professional journey. I loved my music, and yet hated the cold rigidity of those involved in my business. Like anyone in a hopeless situation, I started to become reactionary and once again sought refuge in the more friendly world of contemporary music.

To be fair to EMI, they graciously provided me with a small contemporary recording contract and paid lip service to the release of an ill-fated album called *Let Loose*. Clearly embarking on this venture put the classicists around me into major spirals, and yet again I found myself professionally in a kind of void. I was existing, not developing: just think, if I'd become like those career-hungry types at Juilliard I should have been quite happy at this point.

I think one of the main disillusionments to me was that I realized trying to communicate my love of music to new, wider audiences was unlikely to succeed from the classical concert circuit, and so I built my hopes up with the logic that making records would naturally achieve this goal. Then winning the awards reinforced this notion and thereafter, I started to become regularly featured in the media. All of which led me to suppose I was getting through to the general public. It was of course partially true, but without the selling machine in the same crusading mode all I was doing was selling myself as a personality. Inevitably my new agent was unnerved by some of my thinking and, indeed, the advent of the *Let Loose* direction. He was not an ideal choice to reassure the confused record company, and so an unhealthy stagnation began to set in around me.

Within the company I had a close friend called Barry McCann, who placed himself in impossible positions trying to support me. The contemporary album needed showcasing and my classical agent was hardly the right choice. The record company itself needed to be constantly pursued for promotion, which again I lacked. Barry did everything he could to be that shadow, but the position was far too complex. On the classical front, EMI were dazed and confused. They knew they had the goods in me, but were at a total loss to know how to sell them – given my lack of conformity.

Perhaps I should explain that although the record company is huge, the classical department was quite small with really only a statesman at the helm, a music chief, a product manager and a press officer. If you then consider that virtually all the composers and half their artists are probably dead or unapproachable, and excitement peaks only reached fever pitch if something sold maybe 10,000 copies a year, you might get the picture. Individually they may be great people, but their actions make librarians look like whiz-kids. It's not that it's their fault, just the limitations of the job. Obviously I was a bit of an anomaly, being musically suitable for their attentions and yet favoured by larger media way outside of their spectrum of experience.

Although professionally everything looked roughly on course, in fact we were all heading for an impasse. I had a series of curries and chats with Barry, and then went to see EMI's managing director, Rupert Perry. It was obviously a situation that had to change quickly.

– CHAPTER 3 –

Someone in the Corner

I wonder what your perceptions of a record company boss would be, and whether there is a public stereotype image? I guess I've met a few, but I don't think I could spot one across a room. Probably only the pop promotion and music department staff actually look like the clichés they for the most part really are. EMI boss Rupert Perry wasn't really someone I knew particularly, in fact he'd only been in power himself just over a year. However, in autumn of 1987 the need for a heart-to-heart with someone was getting urgent. The Elgar awards and subsequent releases had not led me towards expanding my classical world, and my frustrations were turning me towards contemporary recordings, which were not doing the job either. In fact, this rising musical schizophrenia was actively troubling almost everyone around me. I knew I needed some help, and yet good advice in the music business is as rare as hen's teeth. Rupert was simply my best option because he had a vested interest in seeing my career stabilise. He's very British and sits behind a large desk like some bright-eyed and bearded mariner. Years of success in the States both perfected his skill at listening and heightened his instincts. He's one of those friendly men you bare your soul to, quite forgetting that under the Home Counties sweater and tie there must be a sharp competitive edge which has placed him in the boss's slot on three separate continents. He gave me his time, and I tried as concisely as I could to condense the main preoccupations in this book (except concerning Villa, because he's into Swindon and therefore has his own worries!). He appeared pleased I'd gone to him rather than have the troubles build up further. I left, not really sure what might happen next, but at least

I'd shared my worries with someone equally entangled in the predicament.

I think it took about a week before Rupert reappeared, talking about John Stanley, who he felt might do the trick – if he could be persuaded. So while I continued the merry-go-round of concert performances, EMI made some initial overtures to this Stanley character. I don't know what was actually said, but it was clear there was a genuine respect and friendship between them – and at least, with mates like Barry McCann also involved, I wasn't going to get ripped off in the way I could if I just wandered off and met with prospective managers on my own. I first met John while he and Barry were having an exploratory lunch in some Italian restaurant near EMI's offices. I had heard quite a lot about him by then and was naturally curious to take a look, so I arranged with Barry to drop by the restaurant to return a cassette. I sat with them and talked for a while, and he wasn't really what I expected. Somehow, with all the success he enjoyed, I thought he'd be pretty flash – you know, the kind of moneyed medallion man. It wasn't the case at all, and he seemed quite normal. He was easy to get on with, but asked a lot of questions. You meet someone for the first time and you realise you're inviting them to change your whole life, and yet you've got nothing to go on at all except instincts . . .

Shortly after that he came over to spend time with me in the Hampstead flat. God knows what he must have thought of the place because it's usually in a serious mess, but we found some seating space and just sat there among the confusion testing each other out. I noticed him checking out my records and books, the things on my wall, the Elgar gold disc (later I learned that he had dozens of golds and platinums for his work in the contemporary music world, but he didn't say anything). That kind of success was, after all, the reason to hunt out a manager, to try and coordinate an artist and record company muddled over my contemporary projects.

In a guarded way I thought it had gone quite well, and certainly there was an air of confidence which was reassuring. He left in his blue Rolls Royce and I thought, that's cool. In a weird way I think if you're playing music or doing art you can in some way measure the amount of communication you are achieving by how much money it is bringing in for you and those around you. I felt pretty good about it, but I learned later from Barry that John wasn't quite as sure. In the end it took about six months of meetings between John and EMI, John and the classical department, and between John and me before arrangements were secure. It always felt positive, but what none of us could have realised at the time was that John wasn't just dithering over my potential with contemporary recordings, he was actually standing back and looking at my career overall and pulling together in his mind what the real potential was for me.

There was a point towards the end of that period where I was out on a UK tour with the Wren Orchestra, playing the *Seasons* in the first half and various contemporary pieces with some of my jazz players in the second. John turned up unannounced at Reading to watch. I think that this night was an important part of his decision. Certainly I've often heard him telling the story concerning an elderly couple in front of him at the show. By all accounts they were quite smartly dressed for the concert and really enjoyed the *Seasons*. I started the second half with quite a brisk contemporary jazz piece on the amplified fiddle and according to him the man carefully took his hearing aid out and placed it in his pocket. Many times since then he's used this as a warning about splitting the musical programme too widely. What I think got to him, though, was that during the encore I played a lighthearted rendition of the BBC *Match of the Day* theme and the audience were all clapping along in time – including the old boy. Very soon after that John started the mission. He felt that concert epitomised the situation with me pushing in much too diverse a way, and yet always just saving the day with my personality.

Once things were confirmed it all began to feel more positive. I don't think any of us were ready for what was to follow, but once you've decided to choose a direction you've got to go with it. I suppose the first real shock was that he felt I should put the contemporary projects on one side for a while and we would jointly concentrate on focusing my classical career: now I knew this area wasn't achieving the personal goals I was seeking, but the prospect of someone with no classical background getting involved did seem strange. However, almost before any doubts had a chance to develop I found we were getting involved in positive top-level company meetings to shape up the future.

About a year before all this I'd recorded Vivaldi's *Four Seasons*, and it was still on a shelf somewhere gathering dust at Abbey Road Studios. At the same time as this renewed tempo within the company I went into studio in order to integrate the developments I'd achieved during the live dates over the intervening twelve months: these changes were at my instigation, not the record company's (as has been fabricated by one or two 'purist' reviewers) and only involved re-recording the slow movements of Spring and Summer with a bit more freedom of embellishment. The record became a target for release in September of '89.

Another surprise was that John elected to withdraw me from all media attention: I'd enjoyed a really good time with pretty much all the press and TV guys, but he explained this was simply hurling me towards being a celebrity of some kind rather than actually converting people to the music I so loved. Somehow an agreement was reached with EMI whereby both the classical and contemporary teams worked in parallel with his office and, magically, a sense of adventure appeared: the classical gang for some reason feeling extra muscle had arrived to help their cause, and the contemporary team rejoicing at the prospect of something new to go for – something with a bit more vibe than just a dance track which would be dead in three months. Looking back on that transformation, it was an incredible swing because the record had still to be released and, after all, there were already dozens of versions of the *Seasons* out there selling in dribs and drabs. Obviously I'd built up a lot of goodwill for myself over the years, but without proper focusing it was like a willing army with no one to lead them to a victory.

My own instincts kept me firmly of the belief that classical music could expand, but I could never get to more than any one concert hall full of people at a time. Ironically, one of the biggest advantages I had over other classical artists was that John had actually come from the contemporary corner: it wasn't just that he brought his own experience and perspective with him, it was that he had this sense of the potential weakness in the pop world. A restlessness, a boredom with the music being sold. Our individual instincts for expanding my world just fell together like two pieces of a jigsaw. I guess this was probably what he was sussing out all those months he was weighing up whether to get involved. The result has been great fun as well as serious business. After all these years of trying to beat down doors and then going home wondering if my feelings were wrong, at last there was someone else thinking the same way. Obviously the kind of success we achieved didn't come without struggles, and during the months prior to the Vivaldi release there were inevitable battles between John and EMI, most notably over the *Four Seasons* TV special, which I will explain in the 'Dual Standards' chapter. We've been sniped at, but we both know what we want and how to get it. Opposition is part of the process. The fact that we won the major television award for that special was sufficient for our self-esteem.

The actual release of the *Four Seasons* coincided with me being away for the vital six weeks on an American tour, so strategy was critical. Really quite big sums of money were risked on the promotion, which ultimately must have been Rupert's decision, and these were carefully used by both classical and Barry's gang on posters, adverts, things like that. A great deal of attention was I think put into reassuring the record shops that everyone meant business. After all, most of them would normally only stock tiny quantities of one or two classical releases. Thanks to brilliantly timed PR, the whole release period stayed sharply in focus – even though I wasn't even in the country – and I gather that as the ball really got rolling the two press offices were in the unfamiliar position of not trying to procure interest, but rather building up lists of approaches to send over to us for decisions. One thing bred another, the PR built confidence, shops displayed more and more copies, the record company believed the impossible – I had gone straight to number one in the classical charts, though that hardly represents huge sales: 15,000 sales in a given year was the equivalent of a Michael Jackson-type record success in the pop world.

I think John was probably most rigid over television exposure: he was adamant we must control the timing of my appearances and certainly, looking back on the shape of that period, there was another major appearance always on the horizon to re-ignite the record company and the shops. The Prince's Trust concert, the Royal Command, the BRIT Awards, our own *Seasons* special, *This Is Your Life*, the chat shows ... The result of this strategy created unheard-of sales for a concerto. I'm not really into statistics, but I've still got a fax telling me of five-day sales of over 45,000 copies just for England, which works out at someone buying the record every 30 seconds of every shopping hour, of every shopping day. You can imagine just how special that felt to me, just seeing that many people getting into it.

I suppose everyone who's written a book and been on *This Is Your Life* is bound to be a bore with their story. It really was a total shock when it happened to me. As far as I was concerned, I'd been told by John that there was to be a surprise EMI drinks party so that Rupert could present the pair of us with double-gold discs: it was to be quite a short affair held in Studio One at Abbey Road immediately after the end of work. The awards were due to us and the location and time were absolutely natural. Afterwards John and I, my girlfriend Brixie and Julia (John's wife) were to have a celebratory curry together and they would drop us back at the flat afterwards – hence the suggestion that we should get a car to bring us to the studios. John had explained that there would be some press there for the awards picture itself, and that the EMI in-house video cameras were recording the speeches, and maybe a short blast on the fiddle if I'd bring it along so they could send the overseas countries news of the latest success. Everything fitted together perfectly, and Brixie and I turned up roughly on time to be greeted by a pretty full turnout of EMI and friends. There was a long table with drinks and snacks, and at the far end was a temporary stage built out of the risers used to place orchestras during recordings. There were one or two big banners and lots of gas-filled balloons with (I think) my name on them. There was all the usual meeting and greeting stuff, and then Rupert got up on stage and summoned us to join him. He talked for a few minutes about the then scale of the success and said nice words about John and gave him his award. I then vaguely remember John making me put down the glass I was holding, and Rupert saying, 'Look into my face, watch my mouth – this is a special award,' or something like that, then I took the plaque and held it up to the clapping crowd. Everyone was really pleased I'd got it, and that seemed cool as most had been involved in the project, but instead of the applause and cheering dying away it got louder – so I thought, 'Keep holding it up and smiling.' What I didn't know was that Michael Aspel and a camera crew had come on stage behind me and he was standing there, Red Book in hand, waiting for me to notice. I was a bit disappointed not to get the book straight away, but he kept hold of it. After that things happened pretty quickly. I remember being worried about whether my great friend David Heath had been invited ... he had been. They kept me well away from everyone and we were rushed off in limos, complete with a production executive and a bottle of bubbly in each car, and once we reached the Teddington Studios even Brixie was marched off – and I was left with a makeup lady in an American camper in the parking lot. John, who (surprise, surprise) had been behind it all, was very briefly let through, just to warn me I might be expected to play an impromptu bit on the fiddle – and the rest lots of you probably saw on the small screen. Only a couple of those in the crowd at Abbey Road even knew about the surprise – it had even been kept from Brixie until the last moment in case it slipped out! Playing the show out with Vivaldi just seemed natural, but actually it prompted yet another surge in the shops. Something like a 250 per cent rise, Barry told me later. Whether you like the programme or not, it was a very special evening for me (the Villa team even tried a disgusting rendition of the *Four Seasons*), and for my family and friends. The actual programme goes by very quickly but Thames lay on a lavish private buffet party afterwards, with no restrictions on the amount of hospitality. The Thames TV team were very sweet about it being *my* party and they even replayed the show for us all to watch – while Jeff Green, Diz Disley, Alec Dankworth and myself had a jam session.

Within a few months I was back with Michael Aspel again – only this time as a guest on his chat show, along with the Princess Royal and Michael Palin. We were still very much in the heat of Vivaldi, but we thought it would be better if I played a portion of my Bruch recording, as it was so beautiful and might give people a break from Vivaldi and something new to listen to. We were right, my old recording shot straight to number two in the classical chart behind Vivaldi, and into the Pop Top 30 – definitely not normal Bruch territory!

We both knew there were a lot of dangers involved in this kind of exercise: my years of playing, of reputation-building were actually placed at risk. Firstly, Vivaldi was essentially considered rather poor taste by the 'purists', and secondly I had engaged a manager from outside of the clan – and thirdly I was just being me. I didn't look at it that way at all. By the age of thirty I had actually received the important classical awards, and if for some reason I just stopped playing I could rest on those laurels just as readily as someone who's played into their sixties to achieve the same honour.

But it's not in my nature to simply cruise and, equally, it's not in my nature to dream of mega fees. The only possessions which really matter to me I've got – thanks to what we've achieved. I have my fiddle, and I have my home – although that is far more dispensable if it ever came to the crunch. What drives me on is the excitement that music can breed; it's the prospect of getting more and more people interested in what I love. Playing safe and hiding within the classical traditions is a much bigger gamble for me because within that route is almost certain death to the spirit. I'd much rather challenge the sleepy system, and at least feel alive and be able to play with conviction: that's what makes it work on stage.

One of the main reasons I was so confident with John was that right from the beginning, when I knew the record company were saying to John, 'If you get involved clean him up,' he was not affected. I'm sure I must have presented him with many dilemmas being as I am, but after looking at both sides of the fence he felt the changes needed to come from within the industry, not me. He's never asked me to change a thing about myself, but he's called on huge sections of our industry, the media, and the public to change – and somehow it's happened. My *Seasons* record has now gone into the *Guinness Book of Records* for spending over a year at No. 1 – indeed, this very year I've seen my records in the unique position of 1, 2 and 3, respectively. Yes, it was a high risk at the time – the risk being whether we could pass the music through the machine and reach the larger crowds. Playing good music itself is never a risk.

Ironically, having achieved the impossible and outsold the pop stars with a straight classical concerto, there was a genuine problem trying to play concerts. The way of the establishment is to book their engagements sometimes years ahead. It's not entirely mad, because getting the correct combinations of orchestra, soloist, conductor and venue often requires working well ahead to achieve the actual package. Before John, my diary was already booked up like that, with dates and fees in keeping with the classical thought-processes and consequently, there were no gaps to cater for the massive new interest derived from the recording success. I think the office gets something like six hundred requests a week in one form or another, and there isn't a real space in the diary for a year or two. It was, and still is, a massive frustration. The actual scale of pressure on everyone since all the success is almost impossible to illustrate, and I only get hints as to just how much hits the office.

From my side, the real struggle is to try and maintain my playing standards in the face of an endless stream of demands. For instance, in many overseas countries the Vivaldi story is still really only just beginning and inevitably, with the success story from places like England, some overseas media become very demanding. Last November I was in New Zealand to play old contracted Brahms concerts, while also trying to cater for the Vivaldi promotion: I got through the mixed week just in time to fly into Australia to give fifty-six approved interviews in five days, only to then have to fly into Tokyo to do the same again. Now, I love meeting people, and most of all performing on stage, which is the one time when I really feel at home. However, that scale of pressure makes daily practice-playing impossibly hard sometimes. The trouble was that it was to be another year before I could get back to Australia, and so we tried to fulfil as much as we could while in that country.

We plan these intense periods to give everyone the maximum possible support – which is just part of being in a successful business. It's hard, but I know that John and his gang are back there making sure that only the right things are dealt with and that the company's sales teams follow up afterwards.

One of the things I've discovered over the last couple of years is that providing you are going forward you can afford to be patient on some issues. Until I'd found my way, absolutely everything felt urgent, needed immediate attention. But now, with the cushion of a certain degree of success, I find it easier to wait. A couple of years ago I was restless over a new contemporary recording – that was one of the main reasons why I wanted John's guidance. It's far from forgotten and plans exist, but concentrating on one thing at a time – particularly if you've got twenty ideas in your head – is a great trick. That's a comfortable part of our relationship, because I'm always full of projects or things people have come up with, and now all I do is talk them through with John and they get whittled down to maybe the most likely couple – which then get explored. Whereas before, any or all of them might have consumed valuable time and interest, and if you become associated with strings of madcap ideas that don't happen, the image sticks and you don't achieve anything. Having someone close who understands really helps. It's a bit like having someone in your corner; you've still got to go out and fight, you've still got to win, but if you've got support in your corner they can pace you through each round.

I think some of the positive vibes I feel now stem from having finally found an outlet for my ambitions – not the sort I so disliked in New York but real, live opportunities to get my music heard in the broadest possible circles. The conspicuous success with Vivaldi has opened up so many new possibilities. Whether record and film company executives are genuinely converted to our way of thinking, or just playing along because things are happening for me, almost doesn't matter. Obviously I'd much prefer it if it were the former, but the net outcome is that we are actually able to take our time and crusade on wider stages than before.

My Brahms recording is a fine example of this: a piece of music I've loved all my life. Making a mass-selling recording while maintaining professional standards is very close to heaven for me, but then to get the opportunity to inject real excitement into everyone's home through a daring TV special is the stuff I've fought for since I started playing. In that sense I'm an extremely fortunate artist. It's hard to guess what the future holds. One of the real glories of classical music is the wealth of material to be discovered, celebrated. One thing you can be sure of – as long as I'm improving my playing and there are audiences to enjoy it, I'll be pushing away to get the music heard by as many people as possible. I'm really not into fixed ambitions in the material sense: right now, with my first real home nestled away in Elgar country, my steady girlfriend and companion

Brixie, our friends, and Villa, I'm quite content. But if John rang up and had this crazy idea to go and spend a year in some obscure part of the globe where some forgotten tribe were found to be into interesting ethnic music, I cannot promise it won't be appealing; it's really down to what excites, and how I can best pass on that excitement to others with my music.

– CHAPTER 4 –

Dual Standards

I guess it must be a human weakness, but we do like things in familiar packages. Brown sauce needs that picture of the Houses of Parliament on the front, herbal tea would look pretty strange in bright red or blue packages, and a bank manager in jeans would certainly divide the customers. The fact that I guess I'm an exception to the rule both helps and hinders my progress.

I really didn't engineer my stage clothes situation. As some of you might have already read in magazines, I had been gigging in the States and had gone back through New York to say goodbye to some friends before a Sunday concert at the Royal Festival Hall in London. I stayed in their apartment, flying back early Saturday in order to rehearse that night. Because of getting up early in the States after a late night out, and then flying straight into work, I didn't even open my case until the Sunday morning – which is when I found I'd left everything I needed in Manhattan. A Sunday in England is not the ideal moment to buy or hire a formal outfit, and so I rushed down to Camden Market in the hope that I might find something secondhand. The nearest I could find was the smoking jacket I'm still using, which was at least black and cost more than I had expected – £25, I recall. Trousers were no hassle, nor was a waistcoat, and I found a white collarless granddad-type shirt which automatically put me into a no-tie situation. Shoes were the biggest problem, but in the end I found some horrible black things that looked pre-Second World War but at least they got me through that weekend. So, as you can imagine, I wandered on stage not at all sure of the kind of reception I would receive. In fact, I got no bad vibes at all and so I simply got stuck into doing the business with the music: everyone liked the show and the critics didn't take me apart. This interested me, because the lightness and freedom to move around in that gear – shoes apart! – was wonderful. Ties, lapels, restricted jacket movements are all hassles fiddlers have to cope with, but having successfully got through a formal concert without such impediments I figured it was worth carrying on. But you can imagine – it became something of a talking point and the process of my being seen as something offbeat started its inevitable journey through both the industry and the media. Once that had taken hold the pinning of trophies and good-luck charms on the jacket didn't really seem any great issue. Certainly, if crystals do attract energy or help, nowhere does a fiddler need it more than on a concert platform.

The haircut thing was actually much more gradual than my album covers suggest. In the summers, when traditionally I don't perform classically, I used to get my hair shaved down to a convict cut because I liked it and also sometimes people reacted as though I was rather suspicious – which was a bit of a laugh. I'd been doing this long before the clothes happening and after that situation turned out the way it did, all the preconceptions that I had to grow my hair before I could perform were re-evaluated. After all, if anything was phoney it was me having to grow hair before I was considered acceptable. I looked at women in the classical world. No one dictated what type of gown they wore or how they selected their hairstyle. Then I looked at the Russian musicians like Boris Belkin, who were then being accepted even though they had totally out-of-date '60s long hair, and I started to think that if you can have that kind of nouveau romantic image, why can't you have any look you feel comfortable with? And so I simply chose to partially grow my hair, selecting a style I liked, just the same as everyone else does in life.

All this aside, maybe being an applauded fiddler from foreign parts like Russia helps get the 'purists' ' attention but in truth, that kind of long hair is absolutely impractical for a fiddler and is actually more open to the suspicion of 'image-making' than having it cut short at the sides to get it out the way! The occasional suggestions that I simply bought the gear and had the haircut to become noticeable, a punk-style fiddler, doesn't really trouble me. I know how it all happened, and the audience has never done anything but support me. It's just a shorthand that newspapers more interested in mass appeal than culture feel they need to use. It's ironic that those very newspapers, although still the big ones, are actually suffering circulation losses to the more culturally attuned ones despite heavy promotional drives. One day it will dawn that you don't have to be an addict to want to hear, read or see culture. Until then I guess we all have to put up with the 'media in the middle' between us displaying all those weird messages they think will make it palatable.

Certainly, after concerts and when I'm with friends, I enjoy a good time as much as the next musician. The dance band era saw lots of rave-ups; jazz, rock and, dare I say it, even the classical crowd enjoy a good time – but inevitably the media enjoy focusing on the apparent contradictions of what they term a punk fiddler. That's cool; it's certainly better copy for them. A second-brass player running amok in a pub, or a lute-player in a punch-up, doesn't really hack it for them.

This entire issue of associations has a bearing on the restricted public vision of the classical world. The notion that because we play dead composers' works we have to look as if we're still attending the funeral is very strange. I'm not advocating that players should be able to wander out on stage in just whatever they fancy or that the formalities of a major classical concert should be destroyed. Remember – I've normally got the best view of you guys and sometimes, on a special night, I look out at the ocean of well-dressed audience and the fact that everyone's gone to that much trouble to get there looking like that actually adds to the buzz of the event. But should the musician's uniform always remain so rigid? If every time you went out with your partner he/she got dressed up like a dog's dinner, it would not only get pretty boring but it would take the edge off those 'special' outings because they will be dressed just the same as the time before, and the time before that too. It's back to the issue of familiar packages.

Let's consider for a moment the environment surrounding opportunities in contemporary music. Now, if you take, say, a young guy in his teens, the starter pack for star entry to the rock world would be a plain white T-shirt, damaged 501 jeans, some form of worn sneaker and the right black leather jacket. This latter needs to be short to offer a sense of long legs and a bum, while hair and facial expressions are worn tousled. After that, it's ideal but not essential for him to play an instrument – or better still, sing. However, if needs be, he can clutch a virtually unheard bass guitar or synthesiser as his visual justification for being there. His record might have his performance incorporated along with many other discreet inputs and even digital samples of earlier artists' best records. His video will feature great-looking models and actors heavily enhanced by a TV commercials director. His promotional interviews are naturally his very own. That might sound very jaundiced, but even those of you who aren't at all interested in pop will know of stories that substantiate this premise. It equally applies to the majority of provocative female singers that would look more at home on *Knots Landing* than a rock'n'roll stage. Just this very year the BRITS Awards on TV saw a tribute to rock enacted by a dancing troupe, working on points like some amateur suburban ballet corps. Absolutely nothing could be further from the essential spirit of rock music than tripping across a stage in satin ballet shoes and a leotard!

What makes no sense at all is that we all see what we want to. Everyone can see that Superstar X isn't actually singing – the mouth isn't working at the same speed as the voice. We praise videos as being brilliant when most of the imagery hasn't even embraced the artist we're praising. Only the deaf would not notice how whole clusters of stars actually sound alike because they are owned/produced by a central entity. We accept, tolerate and by our compliance further this entire movement of creative deception, and yet make severe judgements on the legitimacy of a trained classical performer if he isn't wearing a tie! I've tried many times to come to terms with this contradiction in standards, and can only surmise that pop stars are only granted the same semi-status of, say, a soap star, even if it earns them a fortune.

A classical player is seen to be from a world the majority know little about – alongside surgeons, doctors and bank managers. Now, if you saw your bank manager sitting behind his desk deliberating on your accounts in rave gear I bet most of you would worry; you certainly won't give his judgements the same weight as one looking the part. That's obviously nuts, because he could actually be twice as brilliant as the beer-drinking womanizer down the high street. But it is human nature. Now, I can sympathise with this form of logic regarding professional advisers, who might seriously affect aspects of our own lives. However, to extend this same criteria to the creative arts is lunacy.

Would you extend the same creative tolerance if the young classical hopefuls employed the equivalent machinery? What would the parallel imagery be? I bet you can't evoke too much. Would he have a raunchy girlfriend or something studious in Ralph Lauren clothes and horn-rimmed specs? What would he drive – a black Porsche or some faceless estate? What could he wear? One can only imagine the black suit. Would you believe him if his miming was a bit out, or you heard on the grapevine that he didn't play his own cadenza on the record? So rigid is the curtain of conformity held between the industry and the public that it's actually impossible to consider classical performers as either humans or artists. We simply have not been allowed to become individuals. Even a good satirist or cartoonist would be hard-pressed to give character to a classical musician (except for one or two isolated stars) because there is no working imagery of the individual. Stop someone in the street for an image of a classical player and it will be as a small spot on a large group picture reminiscent of old school photographs. There is nothing at all wrong with the argument that uniformity on stage prevents distraction from the music on offer, but as long as the public's senses are kept this divorced it will remain virtually impossible to build decent followings – even if as an audience we are actually ready and willing.

In its own half-assed way, the business has sensed some of this but the remedies involve breaking down barriers that the classical departments can't bring themselves to attack. The dwindling pop industry, hardened experts at cashing in on anything, have leapt to attention at the thought that there might be a sector of the record market on the ascendant. Hordes of ageing pop stars are earnestly reviewing the prospects of making a recording of great significance; arrangers and orchestras are thumbing through their filling diaries; megastar opera singers are contemplating 'popular' recordings which amount to artistic potboilers in order to catch the market. And a new breed of groomed classical musician is emerging, attempting to second-guess what the public might perceive as the classical muso's kit. Fortunately, although such studied calculations of the classics might win the odd award for style and presentation and even score well for technique, they are unlikely to get close to full marks with the audiences. The record buyer has a staggering sense of what is right. A mediocre recording by a huge name invariably does so-so, whereas a great recording by some lesser mortal can be huge if it gets over the self-appointed 'purist's' wall of defence. It's a historically proven fact that the consumer's taste is extremely accurate, which makes starving them of good classical music, in fact any kind of good music, such a commercial and artistic tragedy.

Obviously, in the last couple of years I've tried to establish a bridge between the music that I love so much and the audiences who, up until that point, had been feeling uninvited. I am conscious that professionally it has been a very dangerous activity for me, particularly when I reflect on the kind of warnings being put to me – even way back at the Juilliard, when I was behaving myself!

Initially, music gave me a way to express my feelings when most of my other emotions were numb. The musical institutions then tried to limit my field of vision, and yet, whenever I did break loose, the audience enjoyed the freedom as much as me. It is not a matter of opportunism, of calculated images; it's simply how I've always felt. When at school I was told one should not do this or that on stage, only to discover the audience actually liked it. That bred real confidence in my own feelings. Just like answering questions correctly in a quiz, it makes you hungry for more.

After the huge confirmation from the public in the last couple of years, I now feel more optimistic that perhaps a cultural change might be feasible.

One of the more significant allies and one which has substantially helped the direct connection between music and the audience has been the media. I'm not so stupid as to suppose that their aims are purely cultural, and so the apparent emergence of myself with Vivaldi's *Four Seasons*, and then Pavarotti with Puccini's 'Nessun Dorma', did provide newsworthy platforms for features. What has happened subsequently is that many publications and programmes have discovered that the public has more than a passing curiosity about the subject, and that it's actually quite good business to favour the topic. After all, classical music has the sort of classy touch both editors and advertisers like.

That general vibe is echoed in the phenomenal range of companies who have made overtures to me concerning advertising campaigns. Lots of suited men in big buildings have toiled for God knows how long coming up with perfect campaigns – all scientifically calculated to appeal to their precise corner of the population. Given that at least some of the bullshit is correct, it's fascinating that approaches in the last year have literally ranged from a world-famous Italian fashion house through to manufacturers of ultra-thin rubber gloves, from cars and drinking chocolate to office equipment. If even just some of these highly-paid agency calculations are correct, the public's interest in classical is much wider than the record industry's. The media has really broken down into two camps: the first, inevitably small but authoritative media, has conspicuously concentrated not on the success of classical sales, but on ringing warning bells as to the destruction of the traditional fabric of that culture.

There have been detailed analyses of the marketing of myself, cryptic warnings of it all being a temporary phenomenon, substantial spreads debunking lady musicians who reveal bare shoulders – naturally no mention of pop singers in mere conical bras or that evening gowns are revealing anyway. One corduroy-clad newspaper did distinguish itself by at least looking in comparative detail at a selection of *Four Seasons* recordings. Given the dozens that confuse the novice customer, that was really constructive but unfortunately – perhaps for fear of looking like they might be traitors to the establishment – they felt disposed to end the review of my recording with the suggestion that if the listener didn't like my image, the record could be listened to in the dark! The general tone of reservation initially aired in this quarter was quite understandable. However, in order to try and wake people up we had to push pretty hard with the initial Vivaldi release, and I'm quite sure most 'serious' commentators must have been sick to death of my face. Unfortunately, as they well know, sometimes you have to rattle the can quite loudly in order to gain the attention of the passerby. That was a real but considered risk to my professional standing – especially so soon after winning the main classical award for my Elgar recording. The media, without perhaps knowing much of my real background and with no sense of whether I'd sold out my musical credentials for cash, quite reasonably feared it was burnout time. Gradually over the last year, as my regular concert work continues, these attitudes have softened. The sales of other less 'distastefully' commercial records such as my Mendelssohn and Bruch concertos pushed through into the really 'serious' category, and even straight concerto appearances such as Prokofiev have been selling out within twenty-four hours. Not sinister evidence for these elitist observers to fear the world is being overrun, but unacceptable human beings all humming the third movement from the *Four Seasons*. Gradually, there is a sense that perhaps new folk out there might just behave themselves in public and be trusted not to bring beer cans and crisps into the concert hall. Being British, there has not been too much of a display of this optimism in these papers – more a reduction in the cynicism.

I guess it must have been hard having branded me temporary trouble only to then discover that major world talents revered in their very pages are still happy to work or record with me. I know when Klaus Tennstedt agreed to record the Brahms concerto with me I felt great. It was a brilliant moment working with such a real master because, yet again, it was confirmation that stepping out on your own, following your instincts, doesn't necessarily mean being an outcast. When the Brahms was finally released it jumped straight to Number One in the pop charts of 800 high-street record shops.

The reception from the other half of the press, the more popular media, was altogether different, altogether more honest; not always welcome, but for the most part unpretentious. These are after all the papers and television shows which actually cater for the general public. Inevitably there was a fair amount of punk fiddler stuff and lots about Villa, and my girlfriend, Brixie, but it was never left at just that alone. When the *Four Seasons* burst into the pop charts, when awards were won, when our own television special strove to break new ground, the actual news of progress was quite widely reported. The TV chat shows, including a large number of children's programmes, deliberately found time to illustrate the fact that audiences were trying to quietly repossess the music from the puritans, even *This is Your Life* replaced their end signature tune with the *Seasons*. These regular indications of classical music's increasing popularity, even though largely targeted at the individual successes of both Pavarotti and myself, actually raised the overall pace of general 'serious' record sales.

Such reporting put the music back into general entertainment circulation. Indeed, I'm sure it must have helped me be voted Show-Business Personality of the Year by the Variety Club of Great Britain, something which appears not to have happened to a classical musician before. Whether or not the 'serious' newspapers' declarations of doubt, or the tabloids' banners of 'punk rules' were correct, they collectively drew attention to this musical option and then, as always, Joe Public made its own mind up and the record zipped past the one million sales mark – directly into the *Guinness Book of Records*. Living in a country swamped with general media, it's sometimes hard to get a perspective on newsworthiness. Your own paper draws one conclusion and you might perhaps see a second opinion elsewhere, but no consensus can really be drawn unless one spends one's day absorbing them all.

It's perhaps more revealing to take a peep overseas, where many countries are only just getting around to our project. As a general rule the territories with uncomplicated media networks and relatively uncluttered views on the arts have embraced the whole thing almost before we could get to them: Ireland, with its love of the fiddle; the Dutch; the Australians; even New Zealand, where it roared up to number three in the pop charts despite the fact they are still waiting for me to get down there to play the piece. Cultural, inquisitive lands such as Japan gave it a short sharp tweak and it rushed straight to classical number one in its first week and was declared a victory – a misconception which took a while to prove. The whole object is to try and reach past the inevitable sales to those already committed, and on to the general crowd patiently waiting the other side of that restricting wall for someone to show the way. In Britain, the record also went straight to number one classically but the record company was not allowed to rest on its laurels and, eighteen months later, it was still number one – but with half my catalogue up there in the charts and the *Seasons* still sitting impertinently in the pop Top 40 and outselling new contemporary releases. That kind of impetus cannot be sustained artificially. Japan, for instance, has reviewed its attitudes, realising that to be blasé with classical number ones isn't the plan, and so now they are looking in much longer, sustained ways. Indeed, their media has coined a collective term for the new blood, the 'Nouvelle Vogue'. The rigidity of formal countries like Germany and the United States, where classical and contemporary record company attitudes rarely meet, has caused much confusion over me. For our part, we know that some will take much longer than others but, in time, all will relax. Generally speaking, the overseas reporting is very much a manner of fascination with the events in the UK. They feature such trendy aspects as they need to attract the reader but they do then turn to relatively serious observations on the changes in attitude. I guess in some way they strike the mid-way point between the two British media factions. Needless to say, the foreign chat shows appear to have a good time when we're together although the language problem does crop up from time to time – fortunately we have that incredible *Seasons* TV special, which gets me out of trouble almost everywhere.

As I tried to explain earlier, the licence afforded contemporary music is huge compared to classics, and the music video world mirrors this well.

We had huge battles with the funding of the *Seasons* TV special. Before John became my manager, the record company and myself had been developing a treatment for a *Four Seasons* film which was really pretty left-field. They had actually started to fund it, and I guess if it had been made it would have enjoyed a sort of cult following. Instead, John stopped everything and together we created the show which you might have seen on BBC. In the pop world six-figure sums are frequently lavished on promos for the single from some forthcoming album, justified purely on the basis it's likely to be the best four minutes of music to show off. With extremely rare exceptions, the lifespan of the single is incredibly short and profits slight, and the moment it loses grace so does the video; the process then maybe is repeated for a second time. Our *Four Seasons* film captured the entire performance plus interview section for the cost of an average four-minute pop promo, and yet you'd have thought we'd asked for the Crown Jewels! We came up with the shape of the show, the BBC commitment, then invited production companies to submit their own ideas upon our theme before selecting the most sympathetic. Having achieved all this we met real opposition from EMI, who felt John had no place getting involved – 'manager get back to your desk' kind of stuff. What they ignored was that John had been trained as a film cameraman and been involved in hundreds of shoots: indeed, the very same company had once hired him as a film director. Both he and I have been sniped at, but we both know what we want and how to get it – opposition is just part of the process. In the end we got it made and as it happens the film won the coveted Golden Rose of Montreux trophy – which, ironically, is now firmly displayed as their company award! Needless to say all we ever received was a fax with the news. That film tried quite successfully to walk the line whereby the music and performance were in no way interfered with but the lighting and editing grammar were more contemporary. Thanks to strong views from the very beginning and sensitive directing from Geoff Wonfor, this was largely achieved: it made it less boring to watch, while not resorting to pulsing colour light shows.

In the course of viewing old TV shows for research, I came across an '80s ITV show called *Strad Jazz*, in which the jazz expert Peter Clayton watched me perform differing styles of music and chatted about my views on this and that. We got into my admiration for Duran Duran's then visual ideas which I admired, and he got me going on visual interpretations of the classics. I played him Elgar's beautiful 'Salut D'Amour', which they then featured in the background to my conversation. This is how I was rambling on, even then:

'I'm very much into the presentation of music, making brilliant videos where things look wonderful and they can get you into it. I'd love to be in a situation where one could make them of classical music like the pop guys do. For instance, in Elgar's piece 'Salut

D'Amour', I'd have this picture of countryside: Elgar was a bloke who always used to get his inspiration from the country. Maybe where the main theme is being stated for the first time, it could just be general pictures of perhaps a railway line and fields and hills and then there would be the same theme again, and maybe it should be more pertinent showing what he's up to, and this time the angle could narrow in to a couple in the field who are having a wonderful time and obviously mean a lot to each other, and generally the scene with even an empty bottle of wine and a finished-off picnic there. Then of course good times don't last forever, which is what Elgar always seems to be saying in his music, and I think then could be the return of the realisation that they've got to part, maybe for good, in the very near future and obviously that brings out even more tenderness and feelings towards each other. Which is what Elgar is all about: he's one of the most tender, personal types of composers there is and I think that it's really important this scene doesn't happen in the modern day, because so much of what Elgar writes belongs to the time in which he was living. It's a lot about the way he feels towards other people and about the human race as a whole. So his generosity of spirit which he's got at that certain moment in the music is tinged with a bit of sadness about the future, and it features in many of his pieces, which is what makes his music so great. Then there is the realisation again that she's got to go away, alternating with the happiness they've got when they're together – and then the film could have the girl leaving, you know, on the train maybe, and the bloke in the field watching the train going away. It's a man's expression of emotion, because Elgar has the sense of reservedness in his expression always, they're the deep feelings tempered with a touch of reservation which is something which is more common with blokes than women.'

Thanks to a lot of people and hard work, my dreams of being able to become involved in what amounts to classical videos or films have been realised. Even down to winning a big award. However, there is a reason I've written it down now, even though I can't play you the piece of music at the same time as reading it. Forgetting for a moment whose words they are and a fairly slight visual storyline, there are some quite careful insights into Elgar and certain of his driving emotions. Even though it was an impromptu remark, crudely sketched out, it provides small markers towards approaching the man's piece of music. Very few audience-friendly signals like this crop up unless you turn to serious bookwork: many years ago Ken Russell used the television medium in his highly individual way to chronicle the lives of some composers for the BBC series *Omnibus*. Though criticised sometimes as being a bit fanciful, he did manage to convey many of the composers' own feelings directly to the viewer – which was rewarding for everyone and one thousand per cent more successful artistically than most university-style programmes on the arts. In the case of Russell's Elgar, the haunting images of the Malvern Hills still cling to his music every time I hear the composition. The entire issue of freeing the imagination, the stigma of classical music, will always depend on the individual. The dual standards that exist for creative licence within classical and pop music are poles apart, and can only be balanced by industries where there are equal opportunities to enjoy and promote both. The only real criteria is that the material should be good.

– CHAPTER 5 –

Little Boxes

I refuse to be put into a little box – in fact, I think little boxes are there to be opened. 'Frankly, I hope both the radio and the talking picture will develop. I should like to use them – any serious artist would. The artist's vocation is to address himself to the masses. What good would an artist be, except philosophically, if he did not show his art to the masses?'

These words were said by the supreme fiddler Fritz Kreisler in 1929. His attitude attracted a lot of criticism from 'serious' critics of the time, who because of his popularity didn't consider him as 'serious' as other well-known players of the day. His sold-out concerts and his recording legacy have proved the snobs wrong and his example is probably one of the reasons why someone like me is accepted today. After all, it would take a particularly dumb 'serious' writer to dismiss my artistic credibility simply because of my popularity, with Kreisler's example from sixty-odd years ago looming in front of them. As it happens, only about two have been stupid enough to do that, and I would like to thank everyone else who supported me when I particularly needed it and didn't then change their opinion of me just because I had a bestseller. Reassuringly, all my musical colleagues say I'm playing much better than when I won all those 'serious' awards and my intention is to carry on that artistic improvement at the same time as communicating with larger numbers of people.

So what are these petty boxes, these restrictions of the mind so attractive to the cultural pedestrian, so offensive to the rest of us? Kreisler's list we can only guess, but this book now gives me a great excuse to list those that most piss me off:

1) Because of the architecture of the home I was born in and the accent of my parents, I should be expected to speak and behave in a certain manner. Indeed, being a 'classical' musician apparently makes it all the more imperative I mirror certain airs and graces. What bullshit. My father disappeared before I was born and I pretty much moved my centre of influence from home to boarding school by the age of seven. Obviously like anyone else I am partly the product of my surroundings, but these have been schools here and in New York, jazz cellars and nightclubs, soccer stadiums and concert platforms, so why should I be expected to try and mirror behavioural patterns I only witnessed for the first few years of my life?

2) A hundred years ago it was considered standard practice, it was simply expected that a solo violinist would enter the spirit of events. Whether it was within a Brahms or Beethoven, they would be expected to write their own solos – cadenzas, suitable for inclusion within the composition, the appropriate spaces being left in the works concerned by the composers. Now it appears it's considered important to always copy a solo from some long-dead fiddler. It is definitely frowned upon to think of actually doing what was intended – that is, to compose or play your own cadenza. Well, with Klaus Tennstedt's support I took the initiative and provided my own work for the appropriate space in the recent Brahms recording with the London Philharmonic. I'm proud of that, and more especially for trying to reinstate what was in fact accepted practice in the days when the actual composers were alive.

3) Women are, within limitations, allowed to wear exactly what they want on the concert platform while the men are all restricted to wearing the same clothes. The dual standards being exercised here are completely wrong and it's no surprise if the audience have a hard time trying to perceive an orchestra as individuals when the management rules that the majority of them have to walk out on stage deliberately dressed to look like each other.

The Cathedrale Stradivarius which shared my world during four important years.

Doug Ellis making me the proud owner of an honorary share in Aston Villa.

With Graham Taylor when he was manager of Villa.

ve just received the BPI Classical Record of the Year from Sir Georg Solti while Noel Edmonds watches.

A milestone: with Vernon Handley, ny conductor, after winning the Gramophone Record of the Year for the Elgar.

Signing my currer record deal with EMI. Left to right Rupert Perry, EMI's managing director; Richard Lyttelton, Preside of EMI Classics; a seated Jim Fifield, World-Wide President and Chi Executive Officer.

Total harmony: The collective team of EMI Holland giving me a double platinum award. Here classical and pop staff naturally unite.

The moment of truth: with my manager, John Stanley, as Michael Aspel delivers his surprise.

John and I with the famed Golden Rose of Montreux for our Four Seasons *film.*

With Brixie in Birmingham after a private concert for the Princess of Wales and her charity.

The film set for the Seasons *special – hardly a standard concert hall.*

As long as it's not a distraction, modern lighting can help a concert's mood.

All concerts were cancelled during the World Cup but when my manager got married a quick 24-hour trip home was planned.

World Cup harmony: me and Brixie in Italy with (back row) Gazza and Chris Waddle, Gary Lineker (seated) and Steve Hodge.

4) 'Serious' rules for the concert stage. It is considered unacceptable to be seen to be enjoying yourself while engaged in your work. Always look like you're dreaming of somewhere entirely different; never, never smile and on no account speak to the audience. Who creates all this bullshit?

5) Tradition has it written that 'serious' classical violinists must be either Jewish or Oriental. This makes it extremely easy for the 'serious' music critic to spot the next generation's suitable stars. If you think that sounds a bit paranoid, try listing the exceptions.

6) Football-supporting, if it must be indulged in, should be restricted to a casual affair with some obviously mega-safe team, ideally with at least one superstar whose name everyone will know. With rare exceptions it's not desirable to adopt anything outside the capital.

7) Vital behaviour for anyone involved with classical music includes showing undying love and respect for the conductor, irrespective of how you actually feel for the man or his skills. All backstage conversations concerning 'serious' music should reinforce your apparent conviction that symphonies, operas and quartets are the essential types of 'proper' music. The matching law of respect if you are a rock musician is to bow at all times to the infinite wisdom of your record producer, despite the fact he has not attended many of your recording sessions. He is your God and even if he drains your project of all individuality, remember you are fortunate to have him touch your career.

8) It is a precondition of notoriety that at some point in your glittering career you must pronounce to the world the secrets of what you're into and make meaningful pleas for all others to follow in order to make the world a better place for us all to live in. If you are unlucky enough to follow another 'star' onto an interview programme and they've just used your cause, it's easy to swap

topics: the critical bit is to try and prove you've become so credible the public will follow.

9) Prerequisites for a good chat-show appearance include a willingness to admit you've pulled through an alcohol problem, which fortunately requires no supporting evidence to evoke the desired sympathy and respect for your honesty, a declared affection for your children which until the '90s you've largely kept a secret, and a suitable repertoire of deserving stories concerning your declared charity. As an extension of this you can allow yourself at least one shit appearance on a mega-charity event. The performance wouldn't get you past the first round of a talent contest, but because you've so kindly given your services no one will criticise you publicly.

10) As your notoriety increases it will become critical that you purchase the correct car to be seen driving and that the clothes you wear make the right statement. Without these fundamentals your shiny career will stall before you make that vital leap towards the establishment: its institutions will remain closed to you.

11) Probably one of the hardest rules to follow after all the years of grafting is to look grateful when someone in a position of power provides five minutes of their valuable time to consider your career prospects and then decrees a route you rejected years ago.

Obviously it's easy to poke fun at the establishment and its attitudes but there are dangers back there. In the pursuit of progress it's all too easy to lose sight of the vital elements that make you different from the next person. There is nothing wrong with learning everything there is to know from the establishment providing you retain your own identity, your own set of beliefs. From letters and backstage conversations I'm conscious that some music students are attracted to the way I've been able to to do things. That's great if it adds extra impetus to their own ambitions, but the raw truth is I've been playing, been learning, for thirty years and modern attitudes alone will never make up for this vital education. If my presence is in any way a model to the next generation at all I would hope it will act to underline that there *is* room for the individual: for the one who feels different from the rest of the pupils. Never feel limited by the imaginations of your teachers. When I look out at one of my audiences it would be easy to see them as a solid wall of opinion, but then I remember how it was my teacher not the audience that objected to my taking off the jacket. They don't all go home to sit reverently by a bust of Mozart and sip small sherries. Their record collections will include jazz, pop, rock; their dark suit will hang near their leather bomber jacket and jeans. The public are never the restriction; it is the limitations of teaching, of established practices that suppress. Learn everything there is to learn but never lose your own vision. It may not be the mainstream approach to music, but there are potentially large audiences for anything played well by those who are visibly into what they're doing. Remember even Kreisler, sixty years ago, saw the fascination of opening up the little boxes rather than being regimented by them. Be yourself – but do it really well.

– CHAPTER 6 –

Lasting Value

Over this last couple of years my somewhat heightened profile has inevitably changed certain things in life. With diary commitments stretching literally years ahead there is no real sense of freedom, and with that kind of workload inevitably the days are all pretty well governed by the usual routine. This being the situation, nothing much has altered – other than the size of venues, record sales and so on. However, it is most noticeable in the day-to-day side of life – shopping, driving around, family and friends. Suddenly you gain a lot of unexpected friends and invitations to events from people you've never heard of before. There is also an underlying expectation that you should have changed in some way, become larger than life.

Between Villa, good friends, curries and home life, there is little danger of heavy-duty changes. After all, the various teachers and advisers in my life have tried without too much success. Whatever you read about me flying around the world, I'm afraid my love of the status game hasn't even grown to the point where I'm interested in acquiring a suitable 'status' car. If you happen to say you've got a BMW there are still a few people in the room who think they are cool. If they ever saw mine that would be another matter. Literally, last time it gave trouble we seriously considered abandoning it where it lay, so to speak. In fact, on that occasion it was outside Birmingham Town Hall where I was doing a gig but unfortunately they didn't want it! It's a good few years old now, and not too many panels or bits are left untouched by adventure. I know traditionally that's one of the very first status symbols to acquire, but it's really not that important to me. After all, I'm overseas so much it would be a real waste anyway.

For me there has only been one preoccupation over these last four years, one dream that never even appeared to get closer whatever I did to try and help it along. That was to own my own fiddle. It sounds a simple and natural aspiration, but it's actually anything but the case. Two almost insurmountable conditions stood in my way – the astronomical costs of great fiddles and the tradition that soloists have to grind away for many years before being considered seasoned enough to earn a really decent income. Because what I do is viewed as such a fine and worthy form of art, it has to be distanced at all costs from commercial considerations. You can actually review a working year packaged with record releases and hundreds of concerts and, if you're really lucky, see a paper income that might amount to roughly the cost of a standard pop video. Once you subtract all your basic needs for the year, buying anything has to be carefully considered – let alone the necessary hundreds of thousands for an important fiddle. However, I'm sure it would not be thought good form to whine on about such topics!

Classical concert engagements don't on the whole make a lot of money for the soloists – 99 per cent of them are promoted by the orchestra, who obviously are more interested in publicly promoting themselves or the conductor, who is basically the star employee of the orchestra. Unfortunately the audiences won't put up with many concerts of just symphonies; they want the personal contact which you can only get with soloists (whose solo line is interesting to distinguish), who project their own character to the audience, rather than sitting in a large group with their back to the audience. Also the ego and self-interest of the conductor and orchestra sometimes prevents sensible or considerate programme planning, with massive works such as the fifty-minute Elgar Concerto being squeezed into the first half so that the orchestra can showcase a symphony in the second. With these artistic/commercial priorities and correctly strict union rules on how much each orchestra player must get, it is obvious for the survival of the orchestra that the soloist should be paid as little as possible. It isn't any better when the shows are put on by a classical promoter. In London nowadays the two major promoters often have a packed house and get away with paying the soloist roughly £250. It takes a lot of skill to play in front of a great London orchestra and to do it once or twice a year would actually be a great success for a young solist – all for £500 a year! That's the situation I was faced with, basically having to pay to play. That would be okay if I had been a typical British/American/Oriental soloist who comes from a family which buys him an apartment and a great instrument to play. Starting off with no money and being totally reliant on my earnings from music put me in a totally different position for a great many years – in the red! It wasn't a good position from which to talk about buying a great violin. In fact, if Charles Beare hadn't heard my playing, believed in it, then lent me a decent fiddle, I would have been playing a cigar box.

It is not a profession one leaps into expecting to harvest easy fame and fortune. Two years ago John and I reviewed this traditional climate for a soloist. I also explained to him the position concerning the fiddle I was using, and all we could do was hope that as a by-product of the massive *Four Seasons* drive I might be able to save money towards owning my own instrument. There is no doubt that with John's experience and my career curve at the point it was, I was in a privileged position compared to most fiddle players facing the same dream – but then the fiddle I was using was a Stradivarius. All the Strads have been given proper names, and the one I used was called the Cathedrale. It was made in his Italian workshops in 1707 and is considered to be from just before his golden period – even the great Antonio had off times. However, when they are right they are something very magical. He was a master at his craft. Every detail was considered, and even the layers of golden varnish were used as part of the tone-tuning process.

It had been evident for some years that I needed to have a 'serious' fiddle, but although there were schemes to enable players of many nationalities, often of average achievement, to play great instruments, there was no such avenue open to me – being British. In the end, in fact in 1987, the Cathedrale was actually bought by a private sponsor who provided me with the free use of it while I, in turn, attempted a repayment scheme, despite a heavily escalating valuation, in order to maybe one day finally own my own fiddle. I was extremely lucky with this arrangement and grateful to that person (hi, and thanks again), who allowed me literally to travel around the world playing something which could just as reasonably have held pride of place in any protected museum glass case.

Living with something that precious opens up whole new areas for concern. For instance, any temperature shift could prove catastrophic to its well-being, so too with humidity. In some places I have to keep the shower running in the hotel room all day just to try and maintain the moisture levels. Hot television studios too can give huge cause for concern. Indeed, travelling itself is fraught with troubles: one time last year I was performing in Honolulu in unusually high humidity levels and then had to make an unplanned flight to Italy to appear on a major television awards show the next day. I was obviously a bit weary, but my main concern was trying in so short a period of time to gradually shift the humidity levels around the fiddle. It flew sealed and the Italian hotel had humidifiers installed and operational many hours before I even landed. Naturally there was yet another environmental shift from the controlled hotel room to the television stage set with all that dry heat and lighting.

Anyway, back to the story. One of the essential conditions for this loan/purchase arrangement was that each year the fiddle would be revalued, traditionally in late summer. Now, I had been paying such amounts as I could manage but as each summer drew closer to the reassessment point tens of thousands of pounds of extra value were loaded on the instrument – effectively pushing it ever further out of my reach. Even in our first year together, when John and I caused the big upheaval with the launch of the *Seasons*, my concert bookings all still reflected arrangements made perhaps two years earlier, and very few people were expecting the sort of record sales he was to target. The position really looked pretty hopeless, and often I would wonder how on earth other fiddlers, perhaps just setting off on that first serious leg in their careers, could ever hope to own a good instrument – if I couldn't with what was happening for me. It gradually became clear that the only way to arrest the runaway valuation was for us to embark somehow on a kind of personal crusade to buy it.

The sum concerned was so great that it could never have been raised from a single exercise and seeking that scale of financial loan, however unwise, would not have been possible without solid evidence of very heavy streams of forthcoming earnings (which I've explained are hardly automatic for a fiddler). Heat was needed. The record had been out a little while and was resting reassuringly at number one in the classical charts. More importantly, our own TV special had also gone out and (combined with a pretty serious PR campaign) the *Seasons* had made quite a big dent in the pop charts. There was general amazement at this because there were already dozens of versions of this music in both the record shops and people's homes, and suddenly the huge numbers of fans buying it didn't correlate with the record company's vision of who might be out there to attract.

Thanks to a convenient gap in the diary we were able to create just over a week of freedom and decided to put together a series of *Four Seasons* concerts – both to celebrate what was happening and at the same time focus on exactly who these fabulous new armies of friends were who were buying my album. Five weeks didn't leave us much time to organise the concerts, and as classical promoters normally work in years rather than weeks John involved Barry Clayman Concerts, who were more at home working with Prince and Michael Jackson. In those few weeks we tried to redraw the guidelines for presentation: we became involved in subtle sound reinforcement to lift and equalise the dynamic levels very slightly without detracting from the natural sound emanating from the concert platform; we introduced a rock'n'roll lighting crew and rig, but then restricted them to just four light changes in the entire concerto. Again we were adopting a sense of pastures new for the professional team.

It was pot luck what concert halls were available at such short notice but fortunately there were some great venues including the Albert Hall. The tickets flew out of the window, which was really good news, but we were far more concerned about the kind of show to put on, knowing that a great many of those coming were first-timers who had more than likely watched the television special. It really matters to me that people enjoy themselves and would want to come again another time, for maybe another work. So between us we decided to light the stage, not as radically as was used on the TV, but giving each season a separate mood. After all, it was no great crime to depict Winter with a blue light. We gave the sound levels a modest amount of support with amplification and, almost as daring for the traditionalist, we lowered the house lights – which might have prevented the endless showing off of Rolex watches, but did at least move the focus of attention to the stage. After all, a bunch of players sitting relatively still for a couple of hours is hardly a natural focal point. Getting trendy was never the intention, but Vivaldi was incredibly powerful in his descriptions of the seasons – indeed, the composition actually falls under the musical term 'programme'. I try to accentuate his feeling, that very bleakness of winter (*The Sankei* in a Japanese review said it much better: 'In portraying Winter, one is able to really get the feel of the icy cold air, and in portraying Summer one can see the glittering rays of sun. In other words, rather than being just a humble, formal concert, his music appeals directly to the listening audience by working sensations within and making the various scenes from the changing seasons come to life'). It therefore didn't feel sacrilegious to cast a cold blue light over the orchestra during Winter – it gave both the audience and, importantly, the orchestra an immediate feel for what Vivaldi was writing about. The offence was naturally logged by a minority of the rear guard.

Well, the concerts were both exciting to give and wonderfully received. We all got to know each other, and everyone went home the better for the event. This was all good business sense, but what really appealed to me was that we were touring just like a rock band. The same lighting and sound man each night, the same tour manager, players and music. It doesn't sound much, I know, but when you're used to different orchestras, halls, music every show and no lights or sound, then you can begin to imagine its charm. After a couple of performances I could hear the players talking backstage among themselves. Everyone was into the experience and it was getting across to the packed houses. We were actually able to develop the music and the staging, comparing notes from the previous concert, refining, improving all the elements an audience deserves but never gets on the cold one-night stands usually associated with the classical world. Yet another barrier had fallen, though sadly my diary is so jammed it can only be a spasmodic approach until these old commitments are worked out. As we'd chosen a pop promoter, lots of pop marketeers tried to suggest souvenir programmes. The establishment equivalent could also see that we might be good business and made offers, but we really didn't want to rip the audience off with endless pages of ads for banking and credit-card firms, aperitifs and fancy watches. What we really wanted to do was to make friends with the army of new enthusiasts now helping us. We wanted to use up the pages talking in straightforward ways about the evening's music; about how John and I felt; about the other records I'd enjoyed. And so we took the unexpected step of publishing our own, which everyone seemed very pleased about – they sold like hot cakes. They also coincided with the influx of book publishing propositions.

As the months went by, the record sales started climbing into the hundreds of thousands and we began to be able to view the prospect of actual income from the album. Unfortunately the same months going by also meant getting ever nearer to the fiddle reappraisal.

The various book proposals were incredibly tempting with the instant promise of lump sums towards the Strad, but the whole exercise of trying to push the restrictive barrier away from classical music placed me in a very vulnerable position. Even the slightest miscalculation would give those we were upsetting justified grounds to get vocal. Some excuse of a book with a trendy, tabloid-type title was just what the 'purists' would have been waiting to see.

The success of the home-grown *Seasons* mini-tour tempted us into looking at an outdoor event in the summer: placed right, it would fall just before the nightmare of the fiddle assessment and at the same time it was a great idea to have something relaxed and informal. From late spring all the newspapers are full of stories of what they term the 'social season' – functions and gatherings where the minority and pushy types merge to be seen and photographed eating strawberries, wearing sun hats and frocks, brushing lightly with the arts. We thought, great, let's just have a large bash in a nice setting, with good hospitality and even better music.

That was the idea for Crystal Palace. Again, a lot of 'purists' started to freak but we pressed on using the same team as in the spring, plus the Chilingirian Quartet – one of the finest in the world. Despite being in the midst of school holidays, the tickets sold very quickly. We had decided on two ticket prices: a general one for £16 – which offered the English Chamber Orchestra and the Chilingirian, including both the Bruch and *Seasons* concertos from me (which amounted, with the other pieces, to roughly four hours of entertainment); and the second was £55, which was for those who actually wanted to simulate the whole summer thing, and we created an entire tent city of hospitality and deck-chairs around the lakeside for the gig. The council were pretty strict about a lot of this and when we sold the entire VIP ticketing from the very first announcement, we went back and lobbied for a licence for more. In the end they granted us four times the original quota which put the caterers into orbit but sadly still didn't mean everyone who applied got tickets. The overall number allowed to attend was subsequently restricted to 20,000, which meant we were quite easily sold out, but then forty-eight hours before the concert came seventeen fresh restrictions – including a ban on all occasional seating, or food and drink being brought in. At that late stage we obviously had no recourse, and braced ourselves for some discontentment. The day came, and it proved to be the wettest of the entire summer! The M25 flooded nearby, it was terrible: there were roughly 600 people working for us that day and John was noticeably ageing under the various pressures. They had created a kind of enclosure for me with a sort of patio garden with tables and chairs and a little bar area to entertain my friends afterwards. There was also this huge American camper which had just arrived from being the location dressing room for some movie star, and the rain just kept hammering on its roof. We waited – Brixie, me and sometimes John and his wife, Julia, who had been organising the hospitality for 2,000 VIPs. It never let up. At various points during the day we had long conversations as to whether to call it all off, but the Meteorological Office kept promising there might be a break coming. The conditions were taxing everyone as soundchecks were vital to the reinforcement crews and naturally, such a massive programme of music needed rehearsal – this was, after all, to be the biggest such event in Britain. Needless to say, the rehearsal like everything else got delayed by the conditions, but eventually we all mustered on a very damp stage and started to run though the Bruch.

Looking out over the vast acreage of prepared arena, it was like a tiny bit of a dream coming true: 20,000 willing fans travelling towards the venue in order simply to drink in good music – I was getting through at last.

Wrong again. As we neared the end of a damp rehearsal of the Bruch there was a restlessness to the side of the stage and, as the rehearsal finished, the orchestra was being commanded off because the three-hour period had elapsed! The fact that we had only been working for twenty-odd minutes and had yet to tackle the main concerto for the evening didn't matter. They left knowing they would themselves now be facing a historic 20,000 audience without a full rehearsal. I was heartbroken and I thought John was going to kill someone. Sometimes the classical world really highlights why it has never made a serious breakthrough. 'Ah!' say the 'purists'. 'Splendid, stick to the rules, that kind of concert isn't on anyway' – but an orchestra and soloist have to be commercial entities, we all have to pay our way because there is precious little out there in the way of financial support. The official three-hour period had elapsed. The fact that the paperwork said rehearsal starts at X o'clock is what counts, even if the weather at that time was so bad it was making the national news. If there was to be a fully-rehearsed orchestra that night, God must move his climatic plans about to suit! Needless to say, we somehow survived the day. Twice John and I walked to the tiny glass window at the back of the bowled stage and peered out at the daunting conditions. How and why so many thousands were prepared to squat on wet grass and mud for all those hours, waiting, I'll never know. All I kept saying was that if it didn't improve I'd go on, on my own in the shelter of the back of the stage and maybe play some Bach solo. Thousands of folk out there for me and the music. It was probably one of the most bittersweet moments of my career. I hope some of you that suffered out there are reading this now, because I cannot really begin to tell you how much that meant to me. I'd have played in the gaps between thunderclaps rather than let you guys down.

The press reports were kind and sympathetic – barring the one inevitable newspaper which had fielded a rather uncommunicative lady who always stood slightly apart from the rest of the media gang and, indeed, visibly smirked at what she clearly felt were the inane questions of the general press. She held her notepad up close to her chin, like she was defending precious answers to an examination or maybe they were state secrets. Towards the end the other journalists were making jokes at her expense, and so she requested special passes in order to cruise with the general public.

Needless to say, hers was the biggest spread – hunting out the disillusioned and rain-drenched at the perimeter gates, where the harsh council rules meant grannies losing Thermos flasks and those frequenting the public catering zone at the top of the hill couldn't hear because of the noise from the catering trucks. Actually, had we wished to place listeners in that place there wouldn't have been a site for the trucks anyway. The irony, missed by the troubled readers, was that that particular newspaper had publicly sponsored and launched an identically-sized classical concert three weeks after ours (with incidentally an £18 ticket base). Sharing the same sales agents, we knew just how few tickets had been sold – in fact, less than 1/20th of what was needed – and we were not in the least surprised when the performer's actual ill-health hastened his withdrawal from the plans.

Anyway, the upshot of all this was that between what we had saved from the concert, and the now rising prospects of a healthy cheque from record sales, we were beginning to group the pennies together. A Ferguson television campaign and eventually this very book deal got us to the point where we could approach the fiddle owner to negotiate. We certainly didn't have anything like enough money, but the pipeline prospects were beginning to make some form of bridging possible. A figure was discussed and eventually agreed which would fulfil my dream – to own my own instrument. There was a lot of back-room stuff still to do to tie up the support I needed, and while we were pressing to complete this the bombshell burst. Not just one of these incredibly rare Strads, but two, were to be auctioned within one week in London.

Naturally, the Cathedrale owner withdrew from our deal and sat back to watch what these comparable violins made at auction. With a recession, and the then shadow of a possible war, there were rays of faint hope and, anyway, Impressionist art only weeks earlier had been a huge disappointment for the big auctioneers. The trouble is that there are literally only 500 of these fabulous instruments in the world, and so a great deal of interest was to be focused on these events. Certainly one of them had been shuffled pretty much around the world on exhibition just to satisfy interest ahead of the auction. We knew we were capable of the preset figure on the Cathedrale, and there was always the off-chance that one of these two might falter in the bidding, and so we arranged that I would be secretly represented at the event. Both John and I were too well known to be seen to be in attendance and so, along with Brixie and one or two others involved, we sat it out in the suite of a private club. The news was not good. The price raced past our figure with four or five bidders in pursuit, and ended some hundreds of thousands higher than we could possibly hope to achieve. Everything was lost. All our efforts couldn't compete with the ridiculous spiral these fiddles are caught in. Naturally my sponsor too had been attending, and in just that space of half an hour the Cathedrale had equally rocketed in value and the previously agreed price of the Cathedrale was history. The days went by and a point was reached where paperwork was emerging for the violin's return to the proper owner. Not only had I lost my dream chance to buy, but I was to lose the fiddle – even to perform on. The final goodbye was to be at the beginning of January. There were not too many hard feelings with my benefactor – after all, I had had unrestricted use of it for four years. No, the tragedy lay within the raw fact that works of art, built to create such wonderful sounds, are being hijacked by investors who are turning them into bank vault items. We had all been dragged into a typically greedy capitalist spiral.

Now naturally we had a real crisis. I could just get away with playing the Scottish National Orchestra dates and then the goodwill would start to run out. I needed a fiddle, and the auctions had just displayed that my spending power was simply not there. Brokers and experts did what they could to find something suitable, but nothing emerged. One faint possibility was something, somewhere in the States. After a great deal of negotiation a fresh figure began to appear for the Cathedrale, but inevitably it was up and, having thought an agreement was locked the first time, this was not the moment to rely exclusively on the deal – even if it could be funded.

The American fiddle proved to be a Guarneri. These violins are not as much publicised, but even more exciting. Giuseppe Guarneri del Gesú was a contemporary of Stradivari and created his beautiful pieces in Cremona, Italy. The choice between these two distinguished makers is a matter of personal taste but most of the players I admire have found it necessary to move on to a Guarneri: Heifetz, Stern, Kreisler and Zukerman all belong to the Guarneri club. This particular example, the Lafont, was called after its first owner in 1736 and was considered good enough to take on Paganini in a playing contest, which Lafont lost but which caused Paganini to claim that the Lafont's sound quality was superior to his own. In 1880 it came into the hands of Adolf Brodsky, and has the distinction of being used by Brodsky on 4 December 1881 to premiere Tchaikovsky's great violin concerto. This particular violin was apparently fabulous and, somehow, pressure was brought to bear and it was flown to my Oslo concert in 1990. It was everything they had said and more – the tone qualities were astonishing and it sounded far more sophisticated. It was even a slimmer instrument than the Strad, and felt more comfortable. The trouble was that it was even *more* than the Strad! Grief on grief: having heard just how much better the Guarneri sounded, the Cathedrale was never going to feel more than second best, despite the ridiculous price tag. Heavy-duty negotiations between John and EMI produced some quite startling earnings, thanks by now to close on a million record sales. Nigel the broker, my lawyer Helen, John's lawyer and bankers also did their stuff and eventually, in a fast-moving chain of events literally unimaginable a year before, I bought the Strad and immediately traded it towards the Guarneri (reflecting the capitalist values of the previous owners, selling it for more than I paid for it!). It was a supreme moment for me: since I was five years old I had been playing violin, I had struggled and achieved most of the conventional high points, and yet it took until that moment to be able to curl my fingers around the neck of a top-quality fiddle and call it mine. There is a long line of thanks here: to John who took up the cause and saw it through to fulfilment; to my ex-benefactor despite the price modifications; to Nigel for finding the beast; to Charles Beare for support through the pressured time; the lawyers; EMI; Ferguson; Weidenfeld & Nicolson for simply being there at the perfect moment; and perhaps most especially to you guys who came to that spring '90 *Seasons* tour, the rain-soaked Crystal Palace, or indeed bought any of my records during 1990. The actual chain of events was made possible simply by those points of success. THANKS.

I guess it makes quite a good little story, but the real topic isn't that the punk fiddler finally got his instrument. No, the real point is if it's that hard for me to try and buy a decent fiddle with all the help and attention surrounding me, what on earth must it be like for others equally in need – musicians who aren't lucky enough to get extended loan arrangements for Strads or happen to be selling a million records in a single year? That's the topic. To witness such astronomical price tags is insanity, and in a just world this process should be stopped immediately. Sadly, human nature being what it is, this must be a pipe dream. I'd love to see artists who buy fiddles selling them on in the course of time for simply what they paid for them – to create a closed community of players, rather than syndicates of bankers and investors, would be great.

However, outside of dream time, what is the situation really like for someone trying to buy a good violin? Obviously Strads and the like are non-starters unless you've got seriously rich friends! That's not to say you can't come across those that look like bargain Strads. It's a real minefield, with dozens of proud owners marching into the big auction houses every week clutching what they believe to be a Stradivarius. Some even have the name written inside, but it's virtually certain it will be a fake because the whereabouts of the 500 known Strads are well established. There has been a marked shift from trying to palm off fake art into doing similarly nasty things to those interested in music. As yet, it's a less suspicious market so the prospective buyers are more vulnerable. There are those violins which have been deliberately distressed to 'age' them; there are those which carry bogus names inside them; even those which have been found with older fronts on in order to suggest they are something that a true expert will instantly know they are not. There really is no safe way to buy such instruments without the guidance of an independent expert such as Charles Beare in London. The likelihood is he'll tell you news you don't want to hear, but it's a lot better than buying a fake for a good deal of money. There is always the chance you will come across an older fiddle which simply cries 'Buy me' and, if it's good for you and not a fortune, you could be lucky. If anyone starts to give you a line about its heritage, or indeed sticks a big price tag on it, get Charles or someone very like him before it's too late. Probably the very best advice is to buy a new fiddle: it may not hold the magic of the more famous old ones, but at least you know what you're getting, and even then it's best to have a good music teacher along with you at the beginning.

During the heat of battle to try and buy mine, John and I talked a good deal about how others might be trying to cope with the same exercise. We studied the prospect of creating some kind of a trust with the power to help suitable worthy situations towards a successful purchase. We didn't actually get very far, but somewhere a way should be found – not actually to go out and simply buy fiddles all over the place, but to help top up the funds of those already trying to help themselves. What's needed is a sponsor, an organisation prepared to assist. If we could find such goodwill and create a system for evaluating cases then the most valuable help available to new, exciting violinists could be brought into action.

I myself have benefited from such help – by being Yehudi Menuhin's first scholarship holder, from the Countess of Munster Musical Fund, from the Martin Musical Scholarship Fund, from Youth And Music, and others who financially assisted my Juilliard schooling and then, of course, the party who helped me through those four years with the Strad. I'd like to try and become part of that chain of encouragement. If someone reading this is in a serious position to help, perhaps we could establish something of lasting value? For my part, I would be happy to consider becoming involved in a special version of one of our own shows, where all the profits might go into a fund for purchases. With my schedule it's not something I would be able to do regularly, but perhaps if sponsors were able to say, match our profits with donations, we would very soon be looking at a substantial fund capable of placing numbers of exciting new artists on the proper road to musical careers. We could make it a really special event, and then watch with pride those we've helped as they help shift the dust from the classical old world. Who knows, it might turn into one of those annual jobs and we could then even showcase the odd beneficiary. I don't know if anyone's ever used a book to float ideas like this, but it's something which has been on my mind since the experience of the last year. It was always something which could have come out in any old interview, but this way I hope I'm able to really show you, through my own nightmares, just how big a crisis these runaway valuations are for everyone, and in particular those just starting out on the real main road to stardom. If you've reached this page, then I know you will have read the background. If you have ideas, just drop me a line via the publishers.

– CHAPTER 7 –

Long-Gone Fathers

I guess most of you know that football is the one thing which really takes me away from music. For years and years it's been my abiding passion. The inevitable clash between the season's fixtures and my ever-swelling performance diary has, I know, caused a lot of people headaches. Even if I cannot get to attend a key game, if the match is being broadcast I will arrange to listen to the transmission by getting someone to hold a telephone receiver up to the loudspeaker so I can sit elsewhere in the world and still enjoy the excitement of the match.

It's unfair that the British game has got such a terrible reputation overseas. Travelling as much as I do, I hear all the time the question, why should I want to be involved in a game so apparently dangerous? They aren't talking about any kind of risk on the field but the crowd dangers, the prospects of being beaten up or worse. Our media and government seem to have no idea of the stigma they have brought to the game around the rest of the world. The key games themselves are naturally all fully reported, and these are read by all the supporters and armchair fans. That's just the same as classical concerts being written up for the benefit of the existing music fans. If someone scores an own goal or a tenor sings something flat, it's only news to those committed followers. For instance, if some mega chandelier fell on the audience in a famous opera house and caused casualties, it would obviously become a major news story. However, were the more sensationalist media to then 'discover' that nearly all opera houses are old and (in order to get extra mileage out of yesterday's story) they find a building expert who says bricks over a hundred years of age have been known to crumble, they could breed news of impending danger to all concert-going opera lovers. Once that momentum is running it becomes cancerous. Obviously no one in their right mind wishes to endanger human life, and tragedies such as Hillsborough leave a deep scar on every supporter – in fact everybody.

The wider damage to the sport is, however, avoidable. When an American comes up to me at a reception and is genuinely amazed that I'm brave enough to attend a game in the light of such tragedies, you realise that their only impression of the game is from the sensationalist reportage. Tragically, such reportage is far too often collated very fast and none too accurately, as for instance with Hillsborough, where the initial shock reportage reached around the globe – and yet the subsequent revelations about the police decisions to herd vast unticketed sections of the crowd hardly got the same coverage. Such imbalances do enormous damage to our status overseas, and are so unfair on the vast majority of British clubs and fans doing nothing whatsoever wrong. I've been going to games pretty regularly for twenty-five years, and only once have I ever witnessed anything dodgy – which was when a bunch of Manchester United fans were going down a passage towards the railway station and met Villa fans heading the other way for the buses: that caused a bit of a stampede. Inevitably that was during the whole period of soccer hooliganism, which I'm sure seeded the idea of troublemaking in a great many minds. During the World Cup in Italy I spent quite a lot of time with the British teams, and most people around them knew vaguely who I was – yet simply wearing the scarf and being British caused real suspicion among some people. Neither the fans nor players deserve to be scarred in this way. *Real* troublemakers and *real* dangers need dealing with firmly, just as the phantom opera-house drama would need investigation.

I think all that stuff about making everyone become registered cardholders before being allowed into a crowd is a tragedy. Can you imagine, if the same ruling were applied to my world – if anybody new to the classical world had to go to a post office, register and hold an ID card, before being allowed to attend one of my concerts? Enormous numbers of would-be new converts to the classics would simply not attend: in time, it would have a major impact on both my career and the public's attitude towards my sort of concerts. Football is a wonderful game, savoured by millions of people – it doesn't deserve the stigma. But it's quite obvious that the kind of 'do-it-for-yourself-and-nobody-else' government that we've had for the last twelve years or so would have no interest in preserving or helping a sport which is so good for the health of mass-consciousness.

My own first attempts at the game were pretty feeble, but a cellist called Colin Carr, who joined the Menuhin School a year or so after me, was really good and also he supported Liverpool – which was in itself impressive. So we used to arrange games during our own time at school. Weekends were one chance, but we also had the lunch breaks and used the forty minutes between 2.00 and 2.40 trying to play games. It meant a lot of running about because there were usually only three or four of us a side, and age discrepancies made it worse – we used to put the little shrimps on the wing. Actually it was quite hard to muster up enough players, because the girls weren't interested and half the boys would have preferred to have been born girls. Still, it was all we had and so it was fine.

My first taste of the real thing was as a result of my older step-sister starting to go out with a lad who supported Birmingham City. They took me along to a friendly game against Hibernian, which I loved. I must have been seven or eight, but I can remember it vividly. Birmingham's goalkeeper was called Jim Herriott and I remember he was from Scotland, and he was actually playing against his old club. I know I was only tiny then but I found it really funny because Herriott let a back pass through his legs to give the Scots a goal. After that I think my next encounter was when we were visiting Brighton and I went to see Brighton and Hove Albion play Oldham Athletic (whom they beat 6–0), but I didn't really want to start supporting them. With the move to

Birmingham I did go to the trouble of finding out about the three local teams – Villa, City and West Bromwich – and would watch their results from school, but at that time it was as much trying to associate with this new region in my life as it was interest in the teams' fortunes.

I guess I was an enthusiast waiting for a team to support. That actually happened pretty quickly after those first two games, through the son of one of my step-father's colleagues. He must have been around sixteen and I was about eight at the time I first walked through the gates of Villa Park. Even just the vibe of the place caught my imagination before the game started. It was actually the first Cup match after controversial Scotsman Tommy Docherty took over the club. The match was against Queens Park Rangers, and in the end it was a 1–1 draw but the atmosphere in the stadium was just brilliant. He'd actually got us seats which was just as well as, standing, I wouldn't have been able to see a thing. I was still in short trousers then, but we were well wrapped up and sitting in the Whitton Road stand – which meant we were actually facing most of the crowd. It was incredible – 30,000 fans in one place, all feeling the same feelings. It was something I wanted to belong to, to join.

Villa's fortunes were a bit mixed at that time, they had gained only fifteen points from twenty-three games, and had just had a scare – resting, as they were, towards the bottom of the second division, with real fears of being relegated. However, they secured Tommy to try and reverse this trend and he brought with him a fighting spirit which itself kindled enthusiasm for players and fans alike. Thanks to this energy he brought, Villa held their place in the Second Division and, in fact, only lost one of the next thirteen games. Duncan took me to one or two more matches (I seem to remember one of them was against Charlton), but I was at school for most of the time. One good thing about supporting that club was that, with Docherty in charge, the newspapers always reported the action so it wasn't too hard trying to keep up from school.

As I got a bit older Duncan would sometimes, in the holidays, let me go on my own. One of the worst things that happened to me around then was that I was considered good enough to be put in the Menuhin School orchestra, and that really messed things up because we didn't finish rehearsals until 12.55 on a Saturday. The moment the session was over I'd drop everything and run: I'd get up to Waterloo station and then finally reach the ground for the last twenty minutes of the game. You know, that's the last period of the game where they open the gates up. I'd be there at the Holt end, out of breath, still clutching the fiddle case, but *very* happy to be part of it all. Although the team wasn't enjoying the best of fortunes, I had become a passionate follower.

Whilst Mum was looking for photographs for this book, she found this little poem which I apparently wrote for the school magazine when I was thirteen:

We'll be Back
What a team is Aston Villa!
We've got Rioch, he's a killer!
Curtis always leads them forward
Though bad tackles put him floorward
Number 7, Pat McMahon,
Shoots as hard as any cannon.

We're warning all the First Division
We'll be back within their vision.
We will win our way to Heaven.
Soon we'll play the Albion.
We'll be back, oh never fear!
Villa's great days are coming near.

Towards the end of my period at the School, both my music and my love for Villa were reaching new heights and, for evidence, I'll return to the device of my school reports:

General: This is a pretty good bunch of reports. In spite of having to keep one eye on Aston Villa all the time, he has had a very satisfactory term.
French: He is getting on very well. I wonder if he could find any French football commentaries on the radio?
English: He is developing his feeling for language and managed to write something worthwhile from bits and pieces that had nothing to do with football.
Art: Nigel still is only interested in his very personal sort of fantasy and Aston Villa.
General: Much of the time he is in a ferment of musical excitement and finds it hard to focus on anything – even Aston Villa. He has thrown his mathematics away and bids fair to do the same with his science.

It's funny writing these out. At the end of each term you always live in fear of what the reports are going to say. As long as it's enough to please your parents that's really the end of your thoughts on the topic. Yet if one could only read them with the detached air of an adult you'd actually read the likely pattern of your life. Certainly the two prevailing passions of music and Villa were amply foretold on those funny little slips of school paper.

Not unnaturally, during the next period in my life, while I was at the Juilliard School in New York, it was much harder to stay in touch with what was happening back home. I used to read the results every Sunday in the *New York Times*, but that was pretty much all I could do. At that time their Channel 13 used to broadcast the more important UK games, but unfortunately Villa wasn't in a strong enough position in the League to justify their games being broadcast. Thoughts of getting home to enjoy things like that were totally out of the question. There simply wasn't enough money. I even spent a Christmas out there when cash was short: actually, that wasn't as miserable as it sounds because I spent Christmas evening with Helen Humes, who sang in the Basie band, playing at a party.

Once back in England I could resume my interest properly. My diary wasn't awash with gigs, so I did have the time available, and with Mum and Duncan living in Birmingham and me then in London, quite often there would be a game in one of the two areas, and Villa Park would entail a night with Mum and Stepdad – plus a good meal, which obviously made those fixtures the favourites.

I wish I could really explain the feelings which make following Villa so special for me. On the face of it, I'm just another male nutcase obsessed with His Side. Obviously that could be part of it, but I couldn't do my job without being fairly sensitive. I rely heavily on getting my own emotions charged up from things around me: like powerful music being hammered out right behind me; strong conductors carrying you along on their waves of enthusiasm; audiences responding to the same feelings you are trying to illustrate. These are the essential ingredients. Soccer is a valuable release from the pressures of my crazy world, but it is far more than that; somehow it reaches that same spot. I'll try and explain. First of all I love the sense of history surrounding Villa. After all, the Club was formed in 1874 and has been a key part of the formation of soccer as we know it today. Along with eleven other clubs it actually founded the Football League. Their very first game was against the local side, St Mary's, Aston Brook. It was their only match of that modest season, and the first half was played under the rules of rugby and the second half under the Association's ruling. Villa won that game and have been thrilling or worrying their fans ever since. In its 117-year history it's actually won the Cup seven times, which is brilliant. There is such a sense of tradition, it's so powerful. You are sitting there watching some game unfold before you and there is this sense of long-gone fathers and grandfathers beside you, sitting in the same seats, watching the same action, sharing the identical sentiments of excitement, of frustration: it is both immediate and timeless. If I'm totally objective about all this, I'm sure having had a disrupted childhood background, and with such a crazy career, the stability of the Club is a really important aspect to me. Whatever happens professionally or privately, the same wonderful rituals will take place every season at Villa Park and I would always want to remain part of it all. It's a sense of belonging that no family upsets or professional crisis can take away from me.

They say that your background, your schooling, all that stuff, moulds how you turn out in later life. Well, I fought like mad all the way through mine not to turn out as other people thought I should and I'm proud of that achievement.

My school was hardly representative of society as a whole – it was full of lucky, talented, protected kids. Even eating chips was some kind of rare privilege because it was all kind of wholemeal bread, brown pastry, brown this, brown that there. Even now, I'm living in a whirlwind of demands and everyone's mustered around supporting and helping me. It's extremely self-centred, an egotist's fantasy. I have to look on this focus towards me as an important part of drawing the high expectations from myself: not wanting to let either myself or those around me down. But if I were actually to try living by those elevated, insular rules I'd probably end up a real sod. Being a Villa supporter, worrying, caring about the same things as 30–40,000 others, is absolutely critical to my own balance. Each of us in the stadium do different jobs, have good or bad scenes going on at home or work, really normal, everyday shit and, for those ninety minutes, none of it matters at all. Any two in the crowd may have differences of opinion, but it will be upon the common topic, and were somebody to call for a Villa cheer then the entire gathering would instantly respond as one. This kind of group consciousness is unbelievably exciting: you really belong.

It's ironic, because although there is this enormous fellowship between the supporters, I do also see a very unwelcome face – the face of change. Up until the 1960s there was the same lasting allegiance between a conductor and his orchestra. The two creative forces bonded together, battling both commercial and professional odds towards common objectives – just like a good manager and his team. In both cases the loyal crowds inevitably appreciated and often benefited from these collective efforts. However, in the 1960s a movement started in classical music which led increasingly towards the conductors becoming not just major earners, but also active players in a game of tactics. They would appear to be quite happy to move their talents to whichever orchestra might offer either increased fees or better stepping-stones to perhaps yet another base a year or two hence. The development of the creative unit stalled with each change; even though one could argue fresh faces brought fresh challenges, the truth of the matter was that neither loyalty nor development of the unit resulted: merely commercial improvement for the opportunist. Unfortunately you don't have to look too far to see the same commercial preoccupations setting in within the world of football, except that is perhaps for Liverpool where the players appear happy to stay loyal to their club and use whatever they can offer towards the common good. It's become all too familiar to see players just begin to improve, to become an exciting part of the team, start paying back to their club for their investment and bang, they're off – moving on, hunting improved fees – because they have started to show signs of improvement, of being valuable. This constantly impairs the growth of a genuine team and alienates the supporters, who want to feel that they know their star players.

Supporting is a serious business and fans accumulate all the tiny bits of information about players – what they drive, where they drink, live, etc., and rapid changes to the key players are disillusioning, distancing the enthusiast and the club. I'm sure one of the reasons Gazza built up such a natural following is that fans felt they knew him, that he could just possibly be sighted in the pub, and might even buy you a pint. He comes across as one of the crowd. If you listen to some of the old boys talking about when they were quite big-time players, they finished a game in front of a 50,000 crowd and then climbed on their bikes or strolled off with the rest of the people. That all sounds a bit romantic now, but they felt they had done their job and simply returned to normal life – a bit I suppose how I feel about being a fiddler. Being precious and swapping allegiances all the time just for self-improvement isn't really being part of a team, using the word properly.

In soccer's very first years as a sport, the only way to swap teams would have been to move to another town. The game actually started during the Middle Ages, when entire communities took part and the aim was to get the ball from one district to another by virtually any means! It was in the Victorian era, when they were all very busy turning boys into men, that the organised game really started – initially in public schools. Easier transportation and a keenness to compete against other schools led to an attempt in 1848 to standardise the rules, but it wasn't until the Football Association was formed in 1863 that workable rules appeared. Then, as soon as competition aspects were introduced with the Challenge Cup, the sport came alive.

Obviously being elected a senior vice-president of Aston Villa, a club reaching back to those historic times, gave me a huge thrill and I'm really proud to be a tiny part of its fabulous history, but I hope in time that I'll be able to bring more to the Club. Naturally I became an easy and obvious publicity machine for them, and I'm sure somewhere back there I'm probably also being seen as potential fund-raising material. But more than that, perhaps in time I will find a way to arrest this gap between teams and their supporters, to prevent the sort of barriers that have so afflicted classical music over the decades. Commerce and ambition can have profoundly damaging side-effects on the very public opinion which creates opportunities. It is possible to walk a middle course.

It's actually perverse to be rattling on about all this when in fact my first personal introduction to the team was the result of me taking the piss out of one of Villa's players! I can't remember exactly when it was, but I was asked to appear on *Desert Island Discs* with Michael Parkinson in the chair and during the show I was naturally asked about Villa, and I started to joke about Gary Shaw – saying that he never appeared to get muddy and could play ninety minutes of football and still walk off the pitch cleaner than me leaving a concert platform! Anyway, a couple of days later I received this message from my agent that Doug Ellis, Villa's chairman, had been trying to reach me. Obviously I thought maybe I'd overstepped things a bit, but I called him up anyway and received an invitation to meet him. In the end he was really great, and so was Gary. They even presented me with an honorary share in the Club. After that they knew that they had a classical fiddler as a serious fan, and a while afterwards I actually played for their testimonial to Nigel Spink. By this point I'd made it to the Directors' Box. Strange, really, because when you're standing down there among the crowd, looking up, you think about the magic of that box and imagine sitting there among the team supremos, and when you find yourself up there you look back down to the Holt end and relive the incredible vibe of being one of the supporters. I guess I must get something from both, in the same way as I do from concert platforms and jazz clubs. They say a leopard never changes its spots! A lion never stops being a Villain.

– CHAPTER 8 –

Peeping Tom

Do you ever read those 'A day in the life of . . .' or whatever they're called, in magazines? They are sort of browse material, a bit like *This Is Your Life*. You give it the first minute or two to see if it appeals, and move on. Seeing as how I consider first thing in the morning extremely uninviting, I can hardly imagine being able to write anything to keep you interested. One or two publishers actually wanted me just to keep a kind of mega diary and produce a 'A Year in the Life of . . .' without actually having to sit down and try to write a proper book. To me that feels like cheating. I'm not sure just how good I am at writing this much on myself, but at least I'm having a go at trying to explain a bit about me and my world. With piles of old school reports still lying about the place from work on the first chapter, I found two English ones for successive terms. The first (just to put the fear of God into my publishers) could only rise to 'A satisfactory term's work', while the other rather lays down the challenge and is perhaps rather fitting – it said, 'Nigel's understanding and use of words are sound. His outlook on the world is, I think, strongly individual and his written work will spring into life if he can put his real self into his words.' Well, I don't know if Selina Vaughan is still around but if she is, I'm sure I'll get a letter! You see, the one thing I really didn't want was some sterile book carrying my name but not my feelings: the way of the star-making machine nowadays almost completely discounts getting to know them – until, that is, there is a divorce, or a scandal. Then naturally we will learn their age, sexual preferences, salaries, locations of 'love nests', all the bullshit – but still no one to get to know.

The reasons people care about public figures like Gazza, Hurricane

Higgins, even Inspector Morse, is that you feel you do know them. You'd feel sorry if you read of trouble in their life, not just exhilaration that finally you know what they earn. Somehow these figures manage to retain their personalities despite the sterilising filter of star status. I know that in the case of Morse, it's really a character and John Thaw might be different, but your instincts tell you surely not; we are so starved of 'real' people rather than stereotypes, that we want to believe. The whole '80s thing about rushing around obsessed with the need to look like you've just edged out creaselessly from between the pages of a Next catalogue was equally sanitising. Shit, once you'd met one or two of those identically perfect people there's a serious need to find a human being, warts and all. I don't think even the cartoonists managed to turn me into a yuppie!

So, to get back to the point I was trying to make, some shiny book about what I did for a year wouldn't tell you anything much about me, just who I'd met and how exciting it might appear to travel a lot. That's part of my world, but not my life.

Mr Publisher was keen I tried to talk a bit about how I practised and, interestingly, two separate film production companies recently asked if I'd be interested in them being a 'peeping Tom' while I prepared for a concert. Maybe that could work. I'll try amalgamating these various facets and actually give you a typical Kennedy day . . . It won't be a particular day, just how I battle to get through them generally. I mean, sometimes they are really quite exotic (like doing private shows overseas, getting a lift on the Queen's Flight, stuff like that), but real life is much more normal.

Given that I'm actually at home, the day would start somewhere around 10 am, maybe a little later if I'm performing that night. In fact, the basic shape of the day will be dictated by whether there is a show: essentially, if there isn't, my practice will be much more arduous. I usually just climb into sweats and then make tea and toast. I try not to open the mail or read faxes, because that immediately puts my mind on other issues – which doesn't help studying.

There isn't the distraction of a newspaper because I don't take one! I don't have a radio either but sometimes, depending on the state of my head, I might put something on the stereo, just for a while. But if for instance I've got a classical concert that night, I'd *never* put on any classical records. Generally, it's much nicer if you can go straight to the music. It's amazing how much less energy you feel if you've been dealing with administration first: you can feel like a teenager if you go to it without distraction, but you soon feel your age if you've been doing all that other stuff and then begin playing. I make the breakfast tea in a huge pot which, after the toast, I then take through with me: it will, in fact, last me through the whole two hours. The actual musical theme for practice will normally be dictated by what concerts are coming up – that is, quite apart from the routine of exercises that I perform. These are very, very simple, and just to keep the technical things working so I won't have to think about them when I am concentrating on more creative work. I guess the exercises probably amount to about a third of my practice period. However, I usually start with something that uses my brain, rather than merely flicking my fingers around. Something like a piece of Bach which I'm working on and thoroughly enjoy playing. It means I'm improving as well as getting myself into the mood for making music. If after that I still find my concentration wavering, then I'd get into a short period of technical exercises before moving on to the actual preparation work for the next concert. I don't prepare myself physically at all. Menuhin used to do a lot of arm-swinging and getting down on the ground and stuff, but I don't find it helps me. One bizarre legacy from school is about half way through the session I'll always want to stop and attend to nature: I guess this is because we all hated the practice work and the only legitimate excuse to stop was needing to go to the loo – where as many of us as possible would congregate for just as long as we dared. I guess old habits and a big pot of tea keep traditions alive!

A great many people do things to relax themselves even before they touch the instrument, but for me it works better if I do have a bit of tension. It's just a matter of how you choose to balance that tension and relaxation. It's something important for both young players and their families to recognise, because sometimes they or their music teacher become too involved in workloads rather than the main criteria – which is the love for music. Quite often at Juilliard I met the parents of other students and there was this sense that their offspring was destined to be a Tracy Austin or Andrea Jaeger. There is a real danger of burnout. You see all these wonderful new playing prodigies on television being acclaimed as the stars of tomorrow, and yet 90 per cent of them you never ever hear of again. They've just been pushed too quickly by well-meaning people or indeed events. The dangers are within the mixture of the actual workload, the responsibilities, and the loss of time which the kid would otherwise use to build friendships and learn how to integrate. So it is the balance within them that suffers first and throws them into such sheltered lives. That may seem okay at the time, but the problems start once the kid is on its own, away from the protection of parents or teachers, and having to deal with everything independently: they may be adult but they haven't actually learned how to cope with things a lot of normal kids would handle quite naturally.

I'd usually finish my first practice session around 1.30 pm. Quite often I'll find the outside world starts to catch up with me after lunch, which can very easily destroy the chances of the other two hours in the afternoon. It really is a very fragile process, particularly if maybe I've had to get involved in telephone work. Sometimes very important issues just have to be dealt with, and there are occasions when I simply have to cancel later engagements in the day in order to reinstate the practice periods. It's not a matter of being precious – there's just no point in trying to be a good fiddler if you're not stretching and improving yourself all the time. As long as I've achieved the first two hours' work it's not the end of the world, but the remainder is important. Generally, I'd go for a run before lunch, which would then take me up to around 3:30 pm. After that I'd be a bit lazy just dealing with some of the phone calls, and then back to the practice. With a bit of luck I'd then be through by dinner. I'm sure the fixation with four hours of workout came from the Menuhin School, where I think there were three to four hours allotted. There, it was very much a matter of you practised enough to ensure you played as well as everybody else; some people needed more, others less. For me, four hours strikes a good balance – otherwise there's a danger of becoming overstressed. A lot of fiddle players get things like tendonitis, but then a lot of them practise for seven hours or more a day. With a fairly busy life it's really tough trying to preserve this time when you know there are two hundred press requests for interviews and television, on top of concerts and touring. The daily routine, wherever I am, vaguely breaks into three sections: the technically basic stuff, the next concert preparation, and then the maturing of some piece. If, as so often happens, the day tightens up, then it is the development of the new repertoire which gets lost. (Interestingly, I learned that Isaac Perlman also moulds his days around four hours of practice, and he's certainly in great shape.) The afternoon session is the time allotted to the basic technical disciplines, which all sounds a bit rarefied. It is vital I keep my technique up to the mark, but I make all this rather boring work easier by watching TV at the same time – it's a bit like a soccer player having to practise certain moves over and over, or a boxer working out on a punchbag: I may need to keep playing the same passage over and over again to bring it up to the correct speed, things like that which demand more of the fingers than of the old grey cells! The TV just helps me get through it all without stopping. I normally watch sports, but a good movie with subtitles is great because you don't have to concentrate on listening to them. It may not be good form to admit this, but the sound of the violin right up against your ear is quite an annoying thing after a while, and it's nice to have some background noise. A by-product of this habit is that I've discovered when there is coughing or a disturbance in the audience I'm not so distracted by the interruptions as many other soloists.

If the day is one with a concert performance then the pattern can be very different. Much will depend on when the orchestra rehearsals are scheduled: it's quite likely there will have been one the afternoon before, but sometimes it's actually in the morning. For the sake of illustrating such a day, I'll presuppose it's one of our own concerts where we usually have the rehearsal and soundcheck in the afternoon. Under those conditions I'd probably get up nearer 11 am than 10 am – just keeping things very steady and undramatic. I'd have my bit of toast, take the pot of tea up to the practice room and give it maybe a total of an hour and a half, which would principally be just the discipline work. By that stage there is no point labouring the evening's material, because it's then a bit late to be trying to evolve the working parameters: it has to have been sorted out before then. After that, I'd dump something in the oven and then set off on my run – this I always try and achieve on concert days, and even if I'm in some vast city my driver will find a park or outlying area. I don't really think about a lot during that forty minutes, just take in what I see and create a steady rhythm. What's nice about regular routes is appreciating the changes you see with the different seasons. The presences or otherwise of leaves, what flowers are growing or dying back, the constantly altering moods in the sky. There is something very reassuring, permanent about the cycles of nature, and it's easy to see why the restless spirits of painters and composers have been so drawn towards the topic.

By the time I get back the food will be ready. There is no great ritual around what I eat, although I don't have any red meat on concert days because I find it feels a bit heavy. It would probably be something like fish or vegetables, together with chips – they're a real weakness of mine, especially with mayonnaise. Depending on the start of any rehearsal at the venue, I might try and get in a short rest – and then off to the job.

Obviously the relationship between myself, any conductor and the musicians is absolutely paramount, and often tested early on by my arriving just as the rehearsal is due to start. The long hanging-about process is really bad news for me: if you have worked with the team before, it doesn't take too long to get back to an understanding, but with a new orchestra, there's a good deal of concentration on discovering where each party is coming from, and what the established goals for the piece are between you. Strangely, within that intense period you all know you're living, and by the end there is often a real camaraderie born out of the pressures; it's a very important moment for me because all the hours and hours I put in on a concerto are alone, when I learn the structure of the piece and draw my own conclusions as to what to bring out of the compositions. But I am just one element within the composition, the performance, and short of keeping a spare orchestra in your front room there is actually no way to pre-fit your own contribution into the total musical setting. I don't actually hear the complete thing come together until we are all virtually on top of the public performance.

Then there is the sound quality of the concert hall, which can vary enormously from city to city. Naturally the rehearsal with an empty auditorium always sounds bigger than with a room full of human beings, but that much you get used to. One of the professional assets John and I have introduced to our own concerts is the discreet use of sound reinforcement, which at least ensures that the same sound levels exist wherever we are performing and any dullness or sound loss caused by the room can be offset on the sound control board.

Immediately after the rehearsal is probably one of the most vulnerable times for me: I'm away from the protected space of my own home or hotel, yet I'm desperately keen not to get distracted. But concerts are inevitably public events and the media need to embrace the proceedings: if I'm at home or in a city for a few days, it somehow works out that I see most of those needing interviews or photos. But if it's a one-nighter then the pressure's really on – there is no way I can cope with encounters before the rehearsal, and once that is over I have to try and retain everything from that session for the concert itself. It's unusual for the press to be prepared to wait until after the concert – and so the game begins. The concert promoters try and exert pressure and inevitably some compromises get struck. It usually takes the form of media attending the end of the rehearsal to snatch a few minutes as it finishes. I actually enjoy talking with them, getting their opinion on what's happening, but they always need a recap on where you went to school, all that stuff, and stories about the success of this or that part of my career. All basic requirements for their piece, yet catapulting your mind miles from where you ought to be at that point in the day. The real hassle is if there are maybe five or six of these – then you've really done damage to your head. Conversely, to decline access all the time doesn't do your career any good and limits the exposure of your belief in what you're doing. The few thousand who will attend the evening event are already at least partial converts to the music, or else they wouldn't be there. Those who don't turn up but are at least interested in reading an article on the subject are always going to be the potential new friends and listeners.

The dressing room is your only refuge as the performance gets closer. Now there is a lot of mystique surrounding this inner sanctum, and I'd love to weave you all sorts of magical stories about what goes on – but I can't. There are a set number of items and facilities always laid on for me: you know a good cup of tea and an egg-mayonnaise sandwich will always be there, whether it's London, New York or Tokyo, but in terms of what I might do or need it's not that rigid. Strictly speaking, no one is allowed in before a show, although Brixie and John and maybe one or two close friends would qualify. Providing the dressing room itself is large enough not to feel claustrophobic, it's fine because each of them understands what I'm going through and will know me well enough to take my unspoken lead as to whether to be fun, quiet, supportive –

the stuff close friends are good at. But there are going to be others local to that city, maybe even working for EMI, who wish to pop in and just wish me well. Sometimes this too is cool, whereas on other occasions it begins to feel like a railway station. It's an impossible situation to predict. It probably has a lot to do with what other pressures you are holding in your head – how the rehearsal has gone, how my private practices on the work have matured, anything and everything comes to bear on that short period of time. All I'm really interested in by that point is making sure I've got a few cups of tea and a little bit of space just to play or merely to sit around doing nothing. It's very different each day – sometimes with a gig it can all go wrong and you don't get any time at all: you have to go virtually straight out onto stage, and yet it works. Other times you've got yourself a whole hour in the dressing room on your own and you just wish there was someone to talk to, despite the fact you've managed to get the place emptied. There really isn't a formula, you just have to duck and weave a bit. Just before the actual concert I'm usually alone, which is great. Anyone who's been backstage with me will have gone forward to get seated and I'll then have a final cup of tea in the fish mug: it's really a green flower vase with a gaping mouth at the top, which I seemed to have acquired somewhere along the way – it's great because it holds a serious amount. *This* is the time when I guess I focus on the task ahead. I think, I pace up and down a bit and become irritated with little things, like my hair or whether my flies are done up. It's when I hear the orchestra start the overture that I really become psyched up. Everything is pushed out of my mind except the music. My main target is to get myself into the mood of the piece. There's no thought at all about remembering the piece – all that's been taken care of over the days of practice. I try and fix my imagination on the most personal moment in the composition, the passage that moves me emotionally the most, and then I'll play that to myself, maybe very slowly: a kind of immersion, taking me as close as possible to the music. Other times I'll just play and replay the opening moments of the music again, just to put me into the same frame of mind. Generally, if you start the performance right it follows on okay because you are then carried by the composition, the orchestra and the physical presence of an audience out there in front of you. Once you're out there everything changes. All the pressures around you fall away and you are just concentrating on the single thing you love most in life: it's like breathing pure oxygen rather than the distressed stuff we generally call air. The only time I really get close to playing music really well is when I can hear the sound of that orchestra behind me. At home I'm just whittling away at it critically, and during rehearsal you are consciously trying to get things to happen that you need to happen for a good performance. During the concert itself it all comes to life and I feel wonderful. There is a release once you step out on stage; it's like walking through some invisible door into a room that feels like your natural home. I suppose it's not that different from going through the door at the Menuhin School, feeling more at ease on the stage without jacket and tie than I did at the School itself. It's the one time when I'm totally myself and no one questions how you're achieving it. It's strange because it is a time of truly intense concentration and yet, because you have done all the homework on the music, if there is a passage when you are not playing the mind becomes remarkably clear; it knows it isn't needed for so many bars, and the sheer momentum of the performance keeps you on target. But sometimes you find yourself stood up in front of seventy musicians playing at full tilt, looking extremely serious, clutching your fiddle while thinking, did I do my flies up properly, or have I left the oven on? Odd thoughts that just pop up from nowhere.

The relationship with the conductor is obviously important and providing you are on the same wavelength over the music, there is this collective energy which breeds, which doesn't just help him and me but the orchestra too. Only twice have there been relationships with which I was uneasy. You still get through the concert okay, but there is no joy in playing under those conditions. You become aware of what's going wrong and you try and compensate for it. It's obvious that with such a problem the players are going to follow the soloist (because they are all trained musicians and they will naturally follow their ears rather than something visual). Ultimately those sort of situations have the potential to become a kind of power game, a musical battle for supremacy, and I think nowadays I know how to win if I have to – but it's really not a situation you ever want to have happen. It's the need to feel safe on stage – which orchestra managers, conductors and soloists all understand – this is the reason why classical bookings do stretch so many years ahead to ensure the right packages of 'talent'.

At the end of the performance I get this brilliant feeling: we've completed the concentrated effort and the audience reaction just washes over you like waves of warm water on a beach. It's a great feeling. I don't know how to write it down, but I promise you it's what fuels you until the next time. All I want to do then is play more – I suddenly feel completely relaxed, obviously warmed up, there is that audience out there calling for more. We've shared something and want to share more ... pure seduction. This is the moment when you have to remember there is a conductor and orchestra on stage with you. They can't be stranded while you waltz off doing your own thing. But I'd play until they stopped asking if I had my way.

But that's not easy with some of today's administrations – one minute over the pre-set hours for the players and someone out front in the box office would be paying out a fortune for use of the extra minutes. It's almost as if the establishment doesn't want uncontrolled growth of interest in classical music. In many ways it's even worse in America – I played a West Coast date recently which was in fact a performance of the Prokofiev First. The concert was really short, but the performance seemed to have gone down rather well – the whole audience was applauding and calling for more; even the orchestra was clapping away. So when I came back out yet again, I gave a short encore which obviously helped fill the evening and at least satisfied the demand for something more, however small the offering. But my American booking agent was there, and the next day sent John the following fax, which I'll quote:

> 'As I am sure you have heard, Nigel had an incredible success in San Francisco. The orchestra loved him, as did the audience.
>
> I just want to point out that Nigel did an encore the night I heard him, and two encores the following evening. With major orchestras in the United States, this is a practice that is severely frowned upon. While the audience enjoyed it, the administration did not take kindly to it. I think this is something you should discuss with Nigel especially with New York coming soon. It will be a huge mistake in New York.'

It would appear I was thoroughly mistaken – I should not have been directing my skills towards a lowly audience, but to some small man who was sitting somewhere with the evening's takings, a calculator and his Rolex chronometer. What absolute bullshit. Of course the agent was merely reflecting the attitudes out there, which must make him very nervous about me. I accept that if the show had been running tight to the American union's three-hour session it might have been irresponsible of me – but that wasn't the case. Indeed, I understand that up until a while ago main East Coast orchestras actually had a clause in their contracts whereby they hire soloists on the strict formal agreement that encores should not be indulged in. Is it any wonder classical music has been kept in the dark ages? Between this obstinate elitism within its fraternity, and downright blindness in the record companies, there was never a chance for classical music to escape. Maybe I am a punk – not the sort the tabloids rant and rave about, but if not being ready to simply toe the establishment line qualifies me, then maybe so. If it's true, I'm bloody proud of it – and hope we continue to stretch the barrier until it snaps.

Once you do get off stage the dressing room fills up instantly, whatever sort of security they try and put in place. Obviously it's a much better moment to say hi to friends, but inevitably you never really get a completed sentence with any one group of people. You suggest one or two might prefer to hang around until the crush has gone, but for me there are two essential ingredients to this period: firstly, I try and insist on getting a beer in with the band. I might be the one out front, but we've all just been through the same nervous tensions bringing the music to life. Everyone on stage is striving to produce their very best and it's great just to have a laugh together once it's finished. It gives everyone a moment to swap stories and joke about the performance – hopefully over things that most people in the audience haven't even noticed. As I was trying to explain earlier, the only time that I hear all my efforts coming together, making a finished picture, is when I'm playing with them. That part of backstage life takes precedence over friends in the dressing room who, if they know me, understand. After that, I always try to sign autographs or at least as many as I can. It is that vital, direct link with the audience that teaches me what they really enjoy and confirms to me what should happen on stage, or be said during interviews: were I just to rely on the profession for my terms of reference there would be no progress. It's great. I try and talk for a minute or two with everyone, and it's amazing just how many young people appear to be studying their music. You can tell it's not just the standard school stuff by the sort of music and instruments they are getting to grips with, and surprisingly large numbers of proper grownups, perhaps not used to queuing backstage, who just want to thank you or from time to time joke about restoring sanity to their households. It appears that one or two youngsters have forsaken their allegiance to some pop star or other in favour of me and, to begin with, the *Four Seasons* or Brahms blasting through the house is considered easier on the parents. (Mind you, I should think that if these kids are anything like true to form, the noise levels may still make the families lepers in their neighbourhood!

By the time I've got through a serious number of autographs, it's usually pretty late and there is a general hustle to get away. Often, I might have to spend time giving an interview and so the night plays itself out. That's not the best way to finish up the night. Pumping a lot of adrenalin during the evening and then going straight home to bed, with maybe an interview in between, doesn't make sleep easy. Instead, what I like to do is go on somewhere – find a music club or something like that, and play the excess out in an informal setting: I guess it's all really a ghost of those aspects of New York nightlife that I so enjoyed. It's as though all the extra encores that I would have wanted to give need to be drawn from me. By that point too I can allow myself a drink of something other than tea!

The after-hours scene is so natural to a musician. It's not an affectation or an urge to be somewhere trendy – it's both a need to wind down and a joy to spend time with other like minds, when most normal people have gone away and left us to be ourselves. In the last couple of years I've had some wonderful times in Ireland playing virtually through the night with local fiddlers and a round or two of drinks. You give so much to each other under those conditions and come away feeling enormous camaraderie, and you're musically very satisfied because you've explored another form of music, someone else's style and taste.

Breaking the classical mould a bit has caused some very strange side-effects, and I guess one of them is the behavioural expectations of a classical player. It's a dumb topic really, because traditionally there has always been a sense of fun with musicians – born, I suspect, partially from what I've just been saying about the need to wind down. You only have to get numbers of them congregating late at night and it will turn into either more playing or party time. The jazz and big band eras are full of stories along these lines, and subsequently there are the legends surrounding the nightlife of rock'n'roll bands. So, being part of a rock band pushing high-energy music out for an evening must leave them in a rare old state. Hence all those famous stories of parties and pranks – things undergraduates do at the end of term without getting noticed, yet put musicians into the national papers.

A rather curious reflection on this stereotyping took place a little while ago in the most traditional of settings, a record company convention. I guess all the delegates had probably been imprisoned most of the week, being filled with optimism and pride about the sundry activities of the company as a whole. Well, there was a gala evening towards or at the very end, which it was hoped large numbers of stars and managers would attend. I was happy to go along because, just like the real value of being able to spend time with an audience after a concert, so too it's great to actually meet and talk with the team who are encountering the retailers. As you can imagine, there was a wide-ranging selection of stars in attendance and the formal part of the evening drifted by very successfully. Once the bosses had done their thing and retired to their rooms, or wherever bosses go, a good time could start, everyone relaxed, and it rapidly splintered into a casual party, spread between three or four adjacent guest rooms. It was fun, but nothing untoward was taking place at all. The interesting aspect was the reactions from the company delegates. Now, I'm sure this was the end of quite an intense week, and naturally such a gathering should bear the hallmarks of a show-business event. The principal contemporary stars who'd bothered to stay and hang out were, at best, reserved and virtually acting as the bosses might have, had they stayed on. You could sense the stalling of what should be a main event to last everyone through the next period of graft, and so between us it livened up a bit. Nothing mega happened – just enough for everyone to go home and talk about it. Now these weren't just classical executives, they were every shade of employee and no one even stopped to consider that Nigel Kennedy, a classical artist, was in the thick of it. It was all totally as it should be, and the only recrimination I heard afterwards was from a pop act who obviously thought that the evening wasn't grown-up enough. It probably doesn't mean much to you, but such a cross-section having a good time (despite the knowledge that we'd all be back in our proper corners the following day) feels great.

Well ... in a vague sort of way I've tried to walk you through a phantom day. There really isn't a bedtime, because I could be out really late, or I might feel it's important to be quiet. If I've just given a concert and I'm doing the same thing again the next night, my bedtime will simply be governed by the success of the concert. On the other hand, if I'm unhappy with my performance, then it's almost certain I'll want to leave early and conserve extra energy so I can squeeze two or three extra practice hours in before the next concert. But if I'm fairly happy with what has taken place on stage, then bedtime will simply be governed by what's going on.

– CHAPTER 9 –

Enter Who Dares . . .

It's fun enjoying the armchair exercise of trying to solve whodunnits, the whole process of being carefully spoon-fed clues and distractions, and then trying to guess the correct conclusions. Traditionally, such adventures follow a well-established line whereby, having seen the crime early on in the story, you then become the silent partner to whomever is investigating the dastardly act. Sometimes we pride ourselves on guessing ahead of the Mastersleuth, but the truth is that without our tame Sherlock Holmes actually asking all the questions we'd be stranded! It is enormous fun working something out ahead of others, but at the end of the day we need a guide to put us on the correct path. Tragically, this fits within my world.

It's hard to imagine another aspect of life so dedicated to isolation, to keeping secrets. Elsewhere I've tried to illustrate the blindness within both the concert establishment and recording professions towards the larger audience that they choose to ignore. Those avenues apart, the only other way open to those interested in exploring the classics is through some form of self-development. However, once one's accepted the sad truth, that there's no one really out there to ask unless you've got perfect neighbours, then there are few options left to you. Increasingly, classically-orientated programmes appear on television varying from pastiches of *Top of the Pops* through to programmes with an audience potential to rival watching paint dry. In between, there are some which really do bring their subjects to life. Quite often these revolve around an insight into a composer rather than a set-piece performance of a work. There is something reassuring about watching and hearing a character going through life, encountering his own highs and lows, using his music to chronicle his experiences. It converts just another recording into something distinctive – a musical sketchbook of events which you yourself have witnessed. Faced with hundreds of years of classical names and music, such programming draws specific composers and works to the fore. Radio, on the other hand, still suffers from time to time from the same malaise as the industry: it provides a splendid service, but mainly for those who already feel confident about walking round a classical record store. So what's left? There is, of course, the occasional classical recording which pops its head up and becomes fashionable, that's a safe-ish bet to purchase. Such rarities apart, there are the classic compilations, which really serve as samplers and do at least give you the proper names for all those familiar passages of music so often used on television commercials and as theme music. That's about the point where it all runs out of steam.

Naturally there are the established record clubs, who do make real efforts to sell their wares with magazines and theme packages. Unfortunately, for many there is a built-in fear of being sold products they don't really want. And so emerges the alternative, of venturing forth to at least partially educate oneself – entering the world of the printed word, and making moves towards a territory which all but needs a translator, so foreign is the phraseology, the classifications. This rigid classification of music into specified groups such as Renaissance, Baroque, Romanticism, Classicism and so on, probably serves music teachers well but does little to persuade the onlooker to look further. However, there is a general aura surrounding such words which feels comfortable – if not in musical terms, at least there is a vague association drawn from architecture or art or literature. With the purest of intentions you might be persuaded to learn more about one period at the expense of the others, only to discover by chance that there is a clear lineage which links music you quite like with another classification altogether within which that style went on to blossom. It would be so easy to choose

:h the Variety Club Show-Business Personality of the Year Award. It's the first time classical music
ned this prize.

Bachelor days in my old North London flat.

*With Klaus Tennstedt when v
were recording the Brahms
Concerto at Abbey Road Stud.*

is photo was taken in 1895, and it shows Dr Brodsky holding the Guarneri violin which is now mine. s great to be part of its history.

My first real chance to use the Guarneri in public – 5 February 1991, in Birmingham.

. . . . . always playing.

and declare, 'Yes, I love Baroque,' only to find the elements you like within it became the real trademark of compositions within Romanticism. Born out of that composer in that time was music which, when united with ideas from another generation, sired a further form of writing.

The classification of music is inevitably an efficient way to fill history books. However, as a method of deducing what you like and what else is likely to be of the same style, it both falls sadly short of the mark and threatens to bore you to death before you ever make a discovery. I'm not a musicologist, nor am I a teacher – I'm also openly biased towards the music that I love. All I can do is try and bring together at least some threads of the variety of music that I enjoy and, by singling out admired composers, view each composer's significance within that time – not just restricting each master to his traditional classification, but also hopefully showing that good music crosses over such manmade barriers. It's bound to be a purely personal view, but surely that's what one's relationship with culture should be about. I hope I can emphasise the value of simply choosing the composer or music that you love, and perhaps exploring that world and influences which will carry you to others you'll enjoy. If you do this, before long it too will turn into a kind of detective game – with musical and historical clues leading you in unexpected directions toward others and their works. It can easily become a lifetime's pursuit – and endless hours of pleasure and satisfaction.

These classifications actually go way back to Greek times, but I'm beginning from the more popular starting point, Baroque, passing through Classical and Romantic to Impressionist, and into the middle of this century. As you know, I hate classifications, so it's not surprising that all the composers I have chosen as the best examples of their respective eras have a depth of communication which far outweighs the importance of the styles of their times.

Period: BAROQUE
Dates: From the beginning of the seventeenth century to about the middle of the eighteenth century
Master: JOHANN SEBASTIAN BACH
Dates: 21 March 1685–28 July 1750

At the beginning of this period in European history, most composers and musicians made a living from employment either within the Church or in Court circles, churning out just whatever their masters wanted, and often doubling up as teachers, gardeners – whatever else helped to make them indispensable. There wasn't a lot of excitement to be had, but the first signs of change started, as did most things during this period, in Italy – with the advent of opera. This at least provided a wider musical scope, and before long these small orchestras were getting chances to entertain in their own right. At that time, virtually everything musical was dictated by Italian ideas – opera, the stunning violin-making going on at Cremona, even the evolution of the concerto itself. There was a general sense of adventure in society, and composers began drawing on Renaissance styles to help show off their keenness to portray more emotion. Before long, however, the dependence on former ideas gradually fell away and the sounds and rhythms we associate with Baroque were formed. There was this shift towards featuring a single instrument to carry a melody whilst the rest of the orchestra supported and wove rhythms beneath and around it. Many of the compositions were rooted in traditional dance rhythms, which at least guaranteed them popularity. Naturally this allowed soloists to become recognised – players such as Corelli and Vivaldi, who (particularly in the case of the latter) made a serious business out of composing and selling this new style to visiting nobility, and indeed getting their manuscripts published in northern Europe.

The musical scene within the other countries could not compete. Back in England, the Civil War had rather taken the edge off enthusiasm for anything. France mirrored Italy – although at least under the Court of Louis XIV the groundwork for some independence was being laid by Giovanni Lulli, even if Lulli was Italian. (It was in that Court, the story goes, that Louis XIV instigated an orchestra uniform, so who knows what he'd have made of me!) Germany too was a spent force to begin with as a result of the Thirty Years' War, which didn't end until 1648. But as time passed it was to be Germany, against the tide of musical events, that would eventually produce the real master of that period – Johann Sebastian Bach.

He was born just after the end of the war, into a family which was eventually to lay claim to literally dozens of musicians. It was also the same year that Handel was born, providing Germany with a second leading exponent of the Baroque style: he was of course drawn towards Italy, but eventually settled in England and became extremely successful. On the other hand, Bach was not a traveller – although he is reputed to have walked over 200 miles to listen to the organist Buxtehude. It's a good story, but a round trip of over 400 miles, through mountains, in November, averaging a minimum of twenty miles a day suggests that he might have got a lift! Bach's actual life story is very straightforward. he lived initially in a place called Thuringia, and at the age of twenty-two married a cousin called Maria – an eventful twelve months, for he gained the job of organist in Muhlhausen, got married, and then, within four months of that, had his first work published – a cantata to celebrate a new town council. It was the start of a long succession of work to impress the musical world.

By his death he had actually composed over 1,500 works. One of the things I really like about the man is that he seems far more interested in the quality and imagination of his music than for any notoriety this work might bring. While many of his contemporaries chased the limelight, he mainly stayed in his home country not just writing these wonderful works but also teaching, encouraging students and acting as the master organist. He and Maria had seven children and thirteen years together before illness struck her down.

He remarried about eighteen months later, this time to Anna Magdalena, the daughter of a Court trumpeter, and with whom he was to have a further thirteen children. Fertile in every sense!

His actual career involved him in employment by Prince Leopold Anhalt, who also played, and for whom he wrote many works. Ironically, Bach didn't think much of the quality of the Prince's organ and so preferred to write for the harpsichord. The story goes that he met Christian Ludwig Margrave of Brandenburg while in Berlin viewing harpsichords, and ended up with a commission to write a set of concertos. It took him some considerable time to accomplish them, in between his work for the Prince, but when they were finally delivered this set of six were to become the perfect example of Baroque – the Brandenburg Concertos, each containing three movements, beautifully balanced, often taking turns to explore differing parts of the orchestra. This period offered a sense of balance and form, together with very strong emotional content. Much of Bach's music was derived from folk origins and yet he had this wonderful inventive, harmonic mind which really deepened the emotional aspects of his music. He simply wasn't afraid to sit down and actually explore harmonies rather than just be content with how it had been up until that point. He was not only supremely musical, but also a fine technician, being able to call on a wide range of devices such as the canon, various forms of fugue, augmentation – whatever he felt right, and yet marry everything together into something which appears both mathematically and musically perfect. The concerto for two violins, generally known as the Bach double, was another definitive piece which I am increasingly performing on stages at the moment.

At thirty-eight he took up the post of Cantor of the City of Leipzig, which involved him in being responsible for a wide range of duties – from being director of church music to collecting firewood for the school. It was here that he was to prove his supremacy yet again to the world. He created the Christmas oratorio, and the breathtaking Passions Mass in B-minor. By this stage the shadows of the Renaissance had become longer and the confidence to explore had grown enormously. There were still legacies within the composers of the time to try and present general emotions as vividly as possible, to establish as clearly as they could the images of celebration, of awe, of excitement rather than private feelings or sentiments. Even at a later point in one of these so-called periods, you can still clearly detect its lineage: were such things possible, you could also look forward in time and see the ongoing effect on future movements.

Bach wasn't just an isolated flash of brilliance. He was born into a tradition of music, he watched and learned from the prevailing leaders of the day, such as Vivaldi, and used his gifts to then make the music, in fact the whole period, his own. It would be another century before others would pick up the baton and run with his musical wisdom.

Towards the end of his life he was virtually blind with cataracts. An operation proved unsuccessful and death came in the form of a cerebral haemorrhage. The standard line is that he was then utterly forgotten until Mendelssohn revived the St Matthew's Passion during 1829 in Berlin, just as the Classical period was dying and the Romantic era being born. In fact Beethoven, born just twenty years after Bach's death, was to develop quietly in the wings – practising Bach, absorbing the genius and waiting to take centre stage himself. So, if you feel drawn towards the mature works of Bach, then it's well worth exploring Beethoven's development.

Period: CLASSICISM
Dates: From the mid-eighteenth century to the first twenty years or so of the nineteenth
Master: LUDWIG VAN BEETHOVEN
Dates: 15 December 1770–26 March 1827

This is actually a period that I don't like very much! The two most famous examples associated with this period are Haydn and Mozart.

Haydn's music is structurally faultless and full of clever, interesting, intellectual ideas. The problem for me is that I prefer to listen to music with soul, and when I listen to Haydn it doesn't seem to be there. As far as I'm concerned, wit and a sharp intellect are not enough to make great music. There certainly isn't the same lack of humanity in Mozart's work, but my problem with his work is that on the classical platform I am playing in the capacity of a violin soloist and I think that the violin concertos he wrote are no better than many works by his contemporaries which have justly been forgotten. It all sounds very nice and pretty, well-orientated towards the technical compositional protocol of the time, but too much like what a yuppie would have as background music for dinner with a few friends! I also think that a lot of the problems as to how this music is perceived might be down to how we hear it performed. A lot of performers don't dare express themselves in this music for fear of being out of style (creating pretty sterile results), and most of the rest are so consciously trying to perform in the actual style of the period, and so proud of it, that the results sound prissy. My disenchantment with this period of music has grown at the same rate as the prevalence of the above types of performance. I certainly don't remember being so dissatisfied with Mozart or Haydn as a kid when I was listening to artists like Menuhin, Stern, Kreisler, Casals, Furtwängler, etc. Anyhow, I definitely feel that the way I would play Mozart would be wrong for the attitudes currently stimulated by present trends, and in turn that these trends are themselves wrong for the deeper, communicational aspects of the music.

At the time that Haydn and Mozart were writing their music, they were part of (or leaders of) a movement which tried to simplify and get away from what was considered the excess decoration and harmonic complications of the Baroque period. Melody and simple chord structures were the order of the day and that, combined with the fact that a lot of the music was tailored for a particularly posy, twee society might explain why it makes such good upper-class muzak! Mozart's great genius did, however, quite often surpass his social circumstance and is obvious in most of his works for piano, his operas and also the Sinfonia concertante in E-flat for violin, viola and orchestra. A most personal, ambitious work which shows us what we are missing in his violin concertos.

That's enough negative shit: what about the bloke who, in my opinion, made the tedious etiquette of the Classical period worthwhile – Ludwig van Beethoven? Ludwig went through a few different styles, but basically he achieved the evolution from the Classical to the Romantic periods. In his earlier compositions Beethoven was influenced by Mozart and Haydn, but quite soon he was achieving better unification of form and depth than his predecessors.

In the middle period of composition, he expanded the depth of communication he was achieving by exploring harmonically and leaving behind the boring harmony concepts of his former influences. By the time of his last compositions, Beethoven had laid down all the paving for the Romantic era.

It quite literally was a cosmopolitan age, with much outward concern for humanity generally. Religion, art, music, literature were all measured by their accessibility and to what extent the works enhanced the well-being of the individual. The rights of the individual were paramount. Indeed, some of this thinking even exhibited itself in the United States, for within this 'period' came the American Revolution and the subsequent birth of the American Constitution. On the face of it, it sounds wonderful, stimulating – an environment which anyone creative would admire. My problem is hardly one of being uneasy accepting the merits of change, but the regulation within the actual output of music. The period may have opened up public concerts, the birth of large orchestras (and somewhere I read a figure of 16,000 new symphonies), but it forcibly suppressed the musical development of emotions, of passion, of real individuality. Sure they all proclaim it's the era of enlightenment, of the individual, but it was the populace they were talking about and not the creative individual. It was a period of massive musical sameness, of subservience to fashion. It was in fact just like that period in modern music when everything you ever heard was a disco recording: same rhythms, speeds, sterility. It was a rigid, ordered declaration of freedoms owing much of its cultural allegiance to the ancient world, while the Romanticism which was to follow referred back to the Middle Ages and more ethnic visions.

The fact that I have a real problem with the hypocrisies of a period that declares freedom and then demands creative limitations doesn't diminish the fact it was a time which witnessed the reign of Mozart and the work of Haydn. If the direct musical output of the period was literally designed not to make demands on these new public audiences, it certainly didn't prevent the seeds of more exciting times being nurtured.

A young Beethoven, aged sixteen, journeyed from his home in Bonn to try and meet Mozart. He was successful, and played for him in Vienna but unfortunately, before much could develop, Ludwig's Mum died and he had to go home and play locally to help with income. As it happens, Haydn passed through Bonn each time he travelled to and from London, and the young Beethoven (now twenty-one) so impressed him that Haydn issued an invitation to return to Vienna with him for lessons. Again, it got messed up by Haydn's return to England, but the composer, in the spirit of these benevolent times, helped Beethoven to continue his development through a series of loans. Beethoven was readily accepted by all circles in Vienna and his resultant work initially displayed the influence of Haydn and Mozart. It was a time when he was still reaching for his own voice.

From the turn of the century until he was about forty-four, Beethoven produced many important and sometimes rather personal works, compositions as diverse as the Moonlight Sonata right through to the majority of his great symphonies – which all bore the hallmarks of the forthcoming Romantic period, and many were sniped at simply because he was exhibiting personal adventure and passions. There was a powerful presence to these works, a restlessness, an apprehension, which contemporary life tried to ignore but which was to fascinate and influence the impending Romantics.

The last period of his life saw him refining all that he had learned – including the famous Ninth Symphony. Compared to, say, Haydn he wrote comparatively little: nine symphonies to Haydn's hundred, but unlike the other composers of the Classic period, Beethoven drew these from deep inside himself – often waging war to capture powerful moods. His progressive deafness must have been unimaginably frustrating, and throughout his life he naturally pursued every avenue for a remedy. The despair he must have felt from time to time, he bore alone – he never married. At the age of fifty-six, whilst travelling back to Vienna, he became ill with pleurisy, dropsy and then jaundice. Every effort was made to cure the great man, but within three months he had died, and the story goes that at that very time of death a huge electric storm dominated the afternoon skies over the city. A fitting, natural finale for a man who had once explained: 'You will ask me whence I take my ideas? That I cannot say with any degree of certainty; they come to me uninvited, directly or indirectly. I could almost grasp them in my hands, out in Nature's open, in the woods, during my promenades, in the silence of the night, at the earliest dawn. They are roused by moods which in the poet's case are transmitted into words, and in mine into tones; that sound, roar and storm until at last they take shape for me as notes.' He was always his own man, which I greatly admire. With centuries of seeing musicians in paid service, often doing extra menial work in order to remain practising composers, Beethoven bucked the system. He produced wondrous works without compliance to public fashions, and died without ever having to write music to another's orders. That strength of character comes out in his compositions.

I've tried to explain the lineage within and between these musical 'periods', and you can perhaps see what I mean. Beethoven's roots were firmly within the influence of Bach, the Baroque, and yet by his death he in turn had helped to give birth to the essence of the Romantics. So, for the sake of this musical progression, the Classicists (about whom I am now supposed to be writing) only existed as a progressional influence for him. I guess if you've read this much of the book you will have gathered enough about my attitudes to detect that Beethoven is my kind of character – prepared to compromise neither his music nor his feelings for the sake of some prevailing opinion. I came across a description of the man the other day by one of his contemporaries, and three sentences within it felt strangely comfortable. They were: 'When he came to us, he used to stick his head in the door and make sure that there was no one there whom he disliked. His clothes were very commonplace, not differing greatly from the fashion of those days, particularly in our circle. Moreover, he spoke a strong dialect in a rather common manner.'

Dear me, how dare a classical musician be NORMAL!!!

Period: ROMANTICS
Dates: From about the 1820s right through to the early years of the twentieth century
Master: JOHANNES BRAHMS
Dates: 7 May 1833–3 April 1897

Of all the musical periods, this is the one I feel most strongly about. The spirit of those times, the music it inspired, are like an extension of my own emotions. Not only is there this general sympathy, but I'm also strongly prejudiced by my love affair with Brahms's violin concerto – which so perfectly captures the mood of both those times and my sentiments. It is one of the greatest compositions from a fascinating musical time. Inevitably it was their rejection of previous influences which helped focus and define what the emerging Romantics were to compose. The rigid disciplines of Classicism which extolled the virtues of control, perfection, tidiness and almost patronised the public with their limits on significant content – this inevitably paved the way for a sizeable backlash. The equivalent virtue of this new movement was to champion and embrace passion, dreams of the unattainable, freedom – even a Romantic sense of isolation. It was a creative licence for the dreamers who had been commercially suppressed throughout the Classic period. It was hardly a coincidence that such sentiments were rising to the surface because for many in Europe those qualities were visibly, literally vanishing from their lives. The Industrial Revolution was rapidly changing the way a great many people lived. Major cities like London actually quadrupled during this century, with the resultant loss of vast areas of open space – people increasingly felt like prisoners. Such huge new populations inevitably introduced crowding and so music, paintings, literature – all depicting rural ideals – became greatly prized; Beethoven's *Pastoral* or works by Turner were an attractive quick fix. Paris suffered the same population surge, and French Impressionists filled the annual salons with evocative studies of rural life – but the desired remoteness, the escapist dreams were actually particularly well suited to the medium of music.

By this stage a great many composers were successfully freelancing, but their newfound commercial position was being sorely tested. The demand for moving, imaginative major works was actually matched by a fast-rising interest in the ballad, which could equally successfully entertain the audience with Romantic notions. It really called for two different musical personas, and for many composers it posed a problem. The larger the scale and emotion of the composition, the bigger the newly-found audiences and concert halls, the more the lone composer felt vulnerable, wished to withdraw – indeed almost become the lone windswept figure being depicted in contemporary paintings. Such was the power being unleashed with this return to heroic dreams, it often led to the formation of small circles of 'like minds', into artistic action groups.

Towards the end of the Romantics it all became a bit over the top, manic in its preoccupations, like some of those vast dark oil paintings of tragic mythology. There was a hopelessness, a sense of souls lost which the Mahlers and Wagners brought. This over-emphasis was to cause the Impressionists to emerge later.

Another quite important musical facet of the Romantics was the return to nationalism – probably again due in part to a reaction to the earlier Classic ideals. Some countries in particular rejoiced in the new freedom of expression through music, which offered outlets for sentiments it was not always prudent to display too overtly. Germany was just such an example, and folk songs became a popular idiom. This popularity eagerly embraced what was termed gypsy music – though it was really an exotic amalgam of nationalities and cultures. The simple Hungarian melodies were popular, infectious and formed the basis of much Romantic inspiration. The actual original songs and rhythms became distinctly prostituted, but the crowd preferred to savour the illusions of ethnic originality. In fact, during the second half of the century it became quite fashionable to enjoy such Hungarian entertainment.

Brahms had a Hungarian friend called Edward, who was also a fiddler, and together they were known to enjoy exploring gypsy music. They toured together, and Edward introduced him to other friends – including Joseph Joachim, who was very successfully in the same line of business. In fact, Brahms had been along to see him play when he visited Hamburg and was riveted by Joachim's performance of Beethoven. They were later to become close friends, and Brahms came to rely heavily on Joachim's opinions.

Johannes Brahms came from a relatively modest family in Hamburg and was the son of a double bass player. Extra income was brought home from them playing together in the pubs around Hamburg's busy docklands. By the age of fifteen, he had given his first solo piano recital, and at twenty he'd sent his work to one of the leading composers, Robert Schumann, for consideration. Unfortunately, Brahms followed this up with a visit to Schumann's home in Düsseldorf – only to find Schumann hadn't checked them out. But he did get an invite in, and promptly blew Schumann and his pianist wife, Clara, away with his playing of one of his own pieces. They became very close and within weeks Schumann was publicly heralding Brahms's genius. Tragically within six months Schumann's deteriorating mental condition reduced him to attempting suicide, and most of his last two years were played out in a mental institution. As it got towards the end, Brahms actually saved Clara any distress by making the hospital visits, and it welded a lifelong friendship between Clara and Brahms – one which has long fascinated biographers: certainly Brahms worshipped her from the beginning, but no evidence suggests either was ever unfaithful to the memory of Schumann. It was in fact the perfect Romantic scenario, right down to the bitter sweetness of forbidden love, and must have fuelled Brahms's composing.

Brahms started writing his first symphony around this time, and shortly afterwards published his own arrangements of fourteen German folk songs, which he dedicated to Robert and Clara. The symphony was neither completed nor performed until eighteen years later – such was his caution over venturing into symphonies whilst Beethoven's work so dominated the genre. Ironically, after all that caution the conductor at the premiere cracked a joke – referring to it as 'The Tenth', implying a continuity with Beethoven. The same man, Hans von Bülow, also came out with the famed phrase 'The Three B's' of music – bringing together Bach, Beethoven and Brahms, which I guess means von Bülow might well have written these last three sections of this book! It's no surprise really; a great work will always rise to the top whatever the period in time.

Joachim kept trying to persuade Brahms to tackle a violin concerto. Like Beethoven, Johannes much preferred to compose while away in the country, and had traditionally turned his summers into rather special holidays for this purpose. The summer following the final emergence of his first symphony he discovered Pörtschach, an Alpine village, which was to become the birthplace of his second symphony. Such was the power of the Alps, forests and lakes that he returned the next summer and composed his brilliant violin concerto. He sent the work to Joachim for criticism, who promptly turned up and they spent some very heated hours exchanging opinions. Being both friends and great musicians, they eventually found the proper balance for what is generally considered a very tough piece to perform. Such was the kinship between them that the solo section, the cadenza (traditionally where the musician gets the freedom to personally decorate with his feelings), was offered to Joachim to compose. That cadenza is still the most widely used whenever the Brahms is performed, the present-day traditionalist naturally insisting it's a fixture. In fact, had Brahms wanted the actual interpretation to be permanent, he wouldn't have offered it out to another fiddler. In my own recording with Klaus Tennstedt and the London Philharmonic, I was given the freedom to provide my own, which, given my love affair with the music, was a magic occasion. So strong are my bonds to the piece that even at sixteen I felt sufficiently at home with what Brahms was describing that I got the first ever 100 per cent in the examination for my London Performing diploma. In my view, we have sadly grown to accept great rigidity, indeed even in our contemporary music, which has become so regimented as to have each piece sound remarkably like another. It is almost a shadow of the same malaise as in Classicism. Perhaps we can look forward to another wave of Romanticism – that would suit me fine.

Period: IMPRESSIONISTS
Dates: Through the last quarter of the nineteenth century to the years following the First World War
Master: CLAUDE DEBUSSY
Dates: 22 August 1862–25 March 1918
Master: MAURICE RAVEL
Dates: 7 March 1875–28 December 1937

When you start trying to look at this period it's easy to get neurotic. In fact, much of the musical output suggests composers were sometimes approaching that state themselves: the dark clouds of Wagner; the changing social and political climates; the ever-expanding sizes of orchestras and markets – all contributed to bewildering activity. The looming shadows of war and tension were mirrored by a much harsher, calculated approach to music with more percussive sounds.

Sheltering within the confusing cross-section of musical adventures, one man, perhaps really two, created their own tiny movement. It was hewn out of their quite separate endeavours and, sadly, its breath was ultimately extinguished by the suffocating forces of the First World War. Fortunately, such was, and still is, the love for orchestral showpieces that their brilliant work survived.

The main man was Claude Debussy, one of the great French composers who single-handedly brought his personal visions to this century's musical stage. Initially, he like so many others felt under the influence of Wagner, but being in Paris at that time fuelled imagination in a way no other city possibly could. It was a time of great artistic and intellectual excitement, where old ways were being questioned in every bar and studio. It was of course the same era as Claude Monet, and it was one of the critics of Monet's painting that coined the term 'Impressionists'. A number of musical reference books parallel the art and music movements (which is loosely true, although generally music periods are later than the art). However, in this case the comparison is reasonable – even down to strange detail, such as it was a critic reviewing his piece 'Printemps' who dubbed Brahms' work 'Impressionistic', and went on to complain that it lacked structural precision and was concerned with musical colour. That a Parisian critic should use such an analogy during the white heat from French painters' movements was hardly surprising. However the essence of what Debussy was trying to break away from was indeed much the same for painters such as Monet. Both were trying to take control, to stand back from the trend to throw every device into the creative process in order to make a statement. Both artists and the one composer, Claude Debussy, strove to stand back and re-establish the specific themes that excited them, concentrating on showing these off, supported but uncluttered. The parallel goes deeper, in so far as anyone lucky enough to have stood before a major Impressionist painting will know that though the main theme will be the play of light and shade and colour, the reason for the painting's success is because it is thoroughly supported with technical skill, draughtsmanship and learning. So too with Debussy, whose preoccupation with colour and atmosphere was perfectly underpinned by an understanding of the formal structures which had been so powerfully used towards the end of the Romantic period. Probably encouraged by endless debates with his intelligentsia friends, he was always alert to new ideas. He was excited by Oriental music he'd heard at the huge Paris Exposition in 1889, which fired his enthusiasm for the subtle use of more exotic colours, and if the term painter could be used for a composer it would certainly fit Debussy. Always ideas were beautifully understated and held a kind of Gallic elegance. The fresh thinking he brought to music, the harmonic and modal system, was of huge importance and virtually all the main composers that featured in the first half of this century drew inspiration of some sort from his talent. Debussy's symphonic sketches – 'La Mer' (completed at a British seaside resort), 'Jeux' (which he wrote for Diaghilev's Russian ballet), and the evocative 'Prelude à l'Après-midi d'un Faune', stand alongside the 'Suite Bergamasque', which includes his much-loved

'Clair de Lune'. And, of course, he enhanced the repertoire for solo piano with some wonderful compositions.

Maurice Ravel was actually a very different character to Debussy. He was a little man, often alone, who never married and indeed spent much of his life taking care of his Mum. Though hardly a recluse, his manner was dry and sometimes brittle to those around him. Not the sort of chap you'd call a close friend – and yet Stravinsky called him one, indeed claiming he was the only musician to fully appreciate his awesome 'Rite of Spring'. None of this would immediately suggest Ravel was a natural compatriot for Debussy's causes. But he certainly was: he had the subtle touch of a master – which he used to fuse together shades of sound. Like some beautiful jigsaw, he made every detail come together to display his imaginary pictures. These attributes also made him a useful conductor, able to attempt the same creative order with an entire orchestra. He was in fact rather more rooted in the Classic traditions, but never suffered from their inhibitions – the telltale signs being a cleanliness of structure, an orderliness. But with it he brought colours and rhythms of great individuality: Viennese, Spanish, jazz, all woven into complex pieces. Ravel also rose to the challenge of composing for ballet, creating 'Daphnis and Chloë' for Diaghilev. He took a keen interest in folk music from a number of countries and, like Debussy and others of that time, was fascinated by all things exotic. At the age of twenty-four, he first conducted his much-loved 'Shéherazade', and virtually thirty years later offered his most famous composition, drawn from nationalistic flavours, 'Bolero' – which created a wide response at its premiere. One lady present reputedly declared aloud that the little man was mad: he nodded. He wasn't very hot-blooded.

During the First World War Ravel was considered too weak for anything more than ambulance-driving (and even then was hospitalised to recover). Much later he was knocked down by a truck which damaged his brain, and an unsuccessful operation closed the story.

The lineage, so distinct in earlier periods, becomes more complex as you move into this century so crowded with styles and changes. It is certain that Ravel, and indeed Debussy, were very smitten with Franz Liszt's 'Fountains of the Villa d'Este' – part of a collection of tone poems published not long after Ravel's birth. Some of his later piano works were also early pacemakers, together with elements of another pianist's work, Frederic Chopin.

As to those influenced by Debussy and Ravel – Puccini, Bartók, Berg, Strauss and many more drew from such ideals. Even those opposed to the cause, like Erik Satie, held Debussy in high regard. Were it not for the all-consuming tragedy of the First World War, one wonders what influence the Impressionists might have enjoyed. As it was, Debussy made his last public appearance in May of 1917 and died of cancer in the March of the following year. Ravel's last few works before he died displayed a return to the security of Classicism. Sadly, the rest of the composers and indeed the general public had their imaginations somewhat numbed by the odour of hatred and death.

Period: JAZZ
Dates: Hard to find a beginning – as with all these 'periods'. Say late nineteenth century. Impossible to end!
Master: MILES DAVIS
Dates: 25 May 1926–

The huge divergence of music that emerged early this century makes attempts at classification quite difficult. My singling out Impressionism stems from my own love for that time, but it was hardly the only movement. Just to take a few examples – Vaughan Williams, Elgar and Holst were all creating their own personal visions within the conventions, whilst the likes of Schoenberg and Stravinsky were developing far more radical approaches. However, just as with previous periods much of the preparation for change had been quietly taking place over decades. Social conditions, political circumstances, reactions to prevailing musical tastes, all contributed fuel. The growth of America, and thus the increase in transport across the Atlantic, added a new dimension.

Since the 1880s music which would later appear as jazz was already being played in the Southern states. In the early years New Orleans, though not by any means the sole centre of jazz, certainly made it feel at home. The raw ingredients of this musical hotpot included elements of local religious music, folk again – just as in the Romantics – and rhythmic influences drawn from West Africa. New Orleans spiced this exotic dish with its French culture, the town itself proving a perfect spot to utilise such portable yet atmospheric music. Parades along the narrow streets became commonplace, and every establishment within Storyville, the 'red light' district, employed a pianist and other players to perform this new music – which was loosely call 'ragtime'. Even funeral processions benefited, becoming musical events. It was a perfect form of music, providing equal opportunities for the front lineup of trombone, trumpet and clarinet as well as for the supporting musicians. It was also possible to play a very wide range of material within the framework of 'Storyville' arrangements.

Although jazz has always remained associated with the town, in 1917 the more sleazy elements of trading in the Storyville area were closed down – spreading the jazz players out. Many were to move to New York, Chicago, Kansas City – places which were to become equally important centres for the music. Within New Orleans the principal, the lead singer/guitarist of his time, was the trumpeter. Players such as Joe 'King' Oliver became real celebrities in the community, as well as taking a powerful lead position in the band, playing the main themes and leaving the other two front-line players to weave and dart colours around his work.

As the 1920s progressed the influence of jazz expanded outside the Southern states. In 1922 King Oliver showcased his New

Orleans jazz in Chicago at the Lincoln Gardens; town after town, jazz stretched ever further north towards New York. The northern music was still primarily variations on ragtime with all its tidy phrases and timing, whereas in the Southern states the individual soloists were beginning to make the music their own. Great players like Sidney Bechet were evolving individual styles and sounds, and it was just two years after King Oliver took his version of New Orleans jazz into Chicago that New York was to witness the brilliant Louis Armstrong join the important Fletcher Henderson band. As a jazz trumpeter he took his natural place as a leader – only his influence stretched way past the band, the city, even the country. He was virtually the architect of the next phase of the development of jazz. No fancy background, couldn't read music, standing among trained New York musicians – and yet the passion and energy he felt conquered everything before him. In the following year many jazz players began to think again about the possibilities of stardom, of bringing what they were feeling to the stage rather than merely performing the more contained jazz. It was into this climate, into this year, 1925, that the great Miles Davis was born in Illinois.

The jazz movement was raging with bigger and bigger bands being formed, arrangers themselves becoming 'names', and the much freer music proving a major attraction to the public – who danced the nights away to the rhythms. Even the white guys were getting in on the act – Bix Beiderbecke, Gene Krupa, Bud Freeman. It must have been fabulous.

The Great Depression naturally had a profound effect on Americans, including their music. Some of the exuberance of the 1920s disappeared and shades of Romanticism appeared to offset conditions just as it had in the early 1800s. The concentration was rather more on the big bands – increasingly white, and the music becoming more sophisticated and subtle, which suited the more cosmopolitan New Yorkers. The star soloists, such as Duke Ellington and Count Basie, were concentrated on the major bands, spreading their style and authority: Ellington heralding 'swing' music, while

Basie simply refused to be held back by the shadow of the depression. By the mid-'30s Fats Waller, the master of stride piano, was capturing everyone's hearts with masterpieces of his own such as 'Ain't Misbehavin'' and 'Honeysuckle Rose', which literally crossed him over into what was the 'popular' marketplace – he was a star, and shrewd musicians such as Basie and the young Miles Davis were taking notice.

Davis, who grew up in a comfortable East St Louis home, not only had this musical backdrop – he had a mother who was a fiddle player, a sister who played the piano, and a dad who was a dentist! Ironically, it was dad who proved the important musical influence, when he bought the thirteen-year-old a trumpet for his birthday and set him up with lessons. The high school band followed, then sessions with an R & B group and a successful meeting with Dizzy Gillespie and Charlie Parker, who were gigging locally with the Billy Eckstine band. The conversations with these two and their music was a profound influence on an impressionable young Miles Davis.

The Second World War, like the First, had a stalling effect on musical developments. Unlike the First, the effect of this conflict was felt within America and at musical levels many of the important performers were called upon by the Services. Needless to say, the music itself remained intact with the big bands of Tommy Dorsey and Glenn Miller working extensively to lift morale. In the autumn of 1944 Davis's father sent him to the illustrious Juilliard School in New York. He had spent the summer months gigging while his mother and father, who had separated, fought over the choice of school he should attend. Davis wanted to be in New York where all the jazz was happening, while his Mum wanted him at Frisk, where his sister was, and could therefore keep an eye on him. His father won, and Davis joined Juilliard – although never finding it somewhere he was to be happy. Maybe a familiar story by now: he spent more and more time in the jazz clubs, eventually travelling back to see his Dad and explaining he was going to leave school.

According to Davis, his dad was cool about his decision and then stopped what he was doing, looked towards the window and said: 'You hear that bird outside the window? He's a mockingbird. He don't have a sound of his own. He copies everybody's sound, and you don't want to do that. You want to be your own man, have your own sound. That's what it's really about. So, don't be nobody else but yourself. You know what you got to do and I trust your judgement.' He then went on to offer financial support until Miles was on his feet. That's the kind of father anyone creative would dream of having, and hopefully Miles Davis's glorious contributions to jazz will have brought his father personal satisfaction. In November of 1945 a nineteen-year-old Davis made a record in a Manhattan studio with Charlie Parker's group. It was a single-day session, and the record was 'Charlie Parker's Beboppers', featuring great Dizzy Gillespie solos and the early signs of Davis's wonderful reflective playing. As the subsequent sessions were made, the growth of 'bebop' was being charted.

The '40s saw a musical search to revitalise the somewhat overweight jazz: a hunt for ways to improvise on a central theme which would challenge and keep the attention of player and listener alike. It was the era of dark glasses, French berets and little meaningful beards. In fact, in the latter half of the '40s there was quite a tussle between this movement and the very reactionary world of New Orleans enthusiasts heavily supporting the likes of Armstrong and Bechet. One way or another it was an excellent time to be a jazz fan.

One of the inspiring aspects of Davis's career is his ability to fully embrace a set of influences and then stand back, distill those aspects he finds rewarding, and them make his own musical statements. The first recordings under his own name started in 1947 in New York but although he had been heavily involved with Parker and Gillespie (who was indeed on these recordings), the resultant style and mood of the music was decidedly Miles Davis. They were fluent, more legato, with Davis playing simple, melodic lines to a musical backcloth of really complex harmonies – sort of musical foils to each other. It was during this year he met the gifted arranger and pianist Gil Evans, and together they spent the next years refining ideas and creating essentially the blueprint for the school of 'cool' jazz with those great collectively-voiced horn sections. Between 1949 and 1953 he appeared to lose all momentum, and for most creative souls that would probably have been the end of the journey. But, as with so many moments in his fabulous career, it was just another beginning – for much had matured from the period with Gil Evans. He enjoyed great success at the 1956 Newport Jazz Festival and began putting together one of his most influential groups – incorporating John Coltrane, Red Garland, Paul Chambers and Philly Joe Jones. This was dynamite – five men full of their own ideas and yet chasing a common goal. So driven were they that a staggering six albums were recorded within a single year. Between them they focused attention on jazz to the extent that large numbers of non-jazz record buyers were taking the plunge. At the end of the '50s the recording group was enlarged to add Cannonball Adderley, which resulted in *Milestones* and *Kind of Blue*, which was probably one of the most important jazz albums ever: its breathtaking rhythm sections and pure beauty of modal improvisation set it apart from all others. The majority of the music recorded was new to the players and the album was almost treated like a recital. Davis was not only back in the limelight but creating the standard by which all others would be measured. It's as though he had withdrawn from the action simply to take stock of his priorities and crystallise them into a single vision.

You read a great deal of complaining about just how complex the world of jazz is to the outsider and how so much has happened in less than a century, but it's actually no different from some of the other movements in music. The real movers and shakers were brought up in one musical environment, coming of age and then creating change. It's actually a constant. Just as Beethoven grew up considering Bach but waiting to be classified as a Classicist. So, too, with Miles – who was born into Louis Armstrong's traditionalist ways and yet grew to shape Cool Jazz and indeed, in his case, other movements too. It's all too easy to simplify and say the 1920s and '30s were traditional veering towards sophisticated, the 1940s and '50s were bebop, abstract in the 1960s and then into the world of fusions.

A familiar pattern reappears with the next significant Davis group, a quintet, evolving during 1963–64 and featuring Ron Carter, Tony Williams, Wayne Shorter and Herbie Hancock, which concentrated on sophisticated improvisational games around familiar standards. The sheer brilliance of the young rhythm section and the fascination of Miles's intellectual exercises earned him enormous respect. It's interesting that back in his days at the Juilliard School when he too didn't feel as if he belonged, he was known to have gone to the trouble of studying scores in their library of works by composers such as Stravinsky, Berg and Prokofiev: his experimentation was always the more assured because of his basic understanding of his craft. Some of his most exciting work from this period was actually recorded as live performances; perhaps his most notable being the 1964 album *My Funny Valentine*. His ideas exposed, he went back to the drawing board yet again and by the end of the decade he was thinking in terms of longer passages of music, still abstracted but now driven by new sounds, new instruments. He had got into listening to records by James Brown, Jimi Hendrix and Sly And The Family Stone. In fact, Hendrix's manager had called him asking if Miles could show Jimi how he played: a request born out of Hendrix's fascination with the *Kind of Blue* album and an urge to use some of these elements in his own work – just as in earlier centuries great musicians from officially differing schools of music were feeding off each other's talents.

His next recordings shocked some 'purists' by embracing rock rhythms, electric guitars and keyboards, even ethnic instruments, but the group shimmered with Davis's usual high standard of players – including John McLaughlin, Chick Corea, Keith Jarrett,

Dave Holland, Billy Cobham, Dave Liebman and others. Naturally with so much new to behold, their work included a lot of experimentation and in just a couple of years they recorded virtually a dozen albums. Miles's capacity to take the highest-quality musicians and explore uncharted regions continues to make him one of the most important musical figures of this century.

We naturally revere the classical masters and their usually linear musical progression, and tend to overlook similar contemporary talents who've dared to explore and still succeed. Often they herald changes within their working lives. Miles Davis has already been at the forefront of music for over four decades, not just as a survivor but as a harbinger of the new.

–CHAPTER 10–

Missing Heroes

The process of writing this book has given me ample opportunities to review those influences which have been brought to bear on my life. Way back last year when we were initially considering likely chapter headings, there was the intention of an essay upon Heroes – the reasons why we need and enjoy them, and whether one can discern anything from the characters of our chosen dreamland gods. At the time it was an interesting idea and it isn't until now that I've thought again about it. To see a pop idol or movie star pinned to a youngster's bedroom wall is virtually a tradition. A special breed of Adonis or slinky blonde serves as a kind of statement of intent – the sort of partner or ideal that appeals. Often it goes further into similar reverence of things such as exotic sports cars or soccer teams.

The sad truth is that given the total freedom to declare my idols, I've never really come up with one. Sure, I fancied being an engine driver but that hardly evoked aspirations to be like anyone else. I think that with the possible exception of a brief teenage moment of reverence for Caroline Munroe decorating the Lamb's navy rum advertisements, I've had an astonishingly dull crop of fantasies.

The problem, and I'm sure it's suitably revealing about me as a bloke, is that my idols were horribly logical. No heroic types such as James Bond or the sullen powers of James Dean, nor was the lure of celluloid temptresses that appealing. In my case I've always played very safe, growing to admire someone with whom I'm already in working contact and, not surprisingly, these were individuals such as Sir Yehudi Menuhin and Stephane Grappelli. It was as though for me fantasy time didn't exist. Stephane really was someone I idolised from the moment we met, which would have been when I was about fourteen. I think there were two main reasons why I so looked up to him: firstly, he played the violin in a way I'd never heard before because I'd been accustomed to only hearing it classically. Obviously I was by that point well into jazz but never using the fiddle as the main instrument. Then there was his lifestyle, which was so different from that of any classical musician I knew: he could have such a good time in the daytime messing around, doing just what he wanted, and yet at night he would just get up there on stage and play brilliantly. He would simply respond to every occasion with so much spontaneity and style. I suppose he represented a possible antidote to the inevitable boredom at school.

I know it would be reasonable to expect me to volunteer certain film stars as heroes but in truth, with the rules at the Menuhin School, we didn't even get to the movies; just television was allowed and we would only be permitted to watch at certain times – after six o'clock in the evening at weekends. Writing this down makes it all sound like a monastery, and I suppose in many ways it probably was a bit. When I was really small I would enjoy reading comics, following week after week the adventures of the various characters, but inevitably you grow out of cartoon strips quite quickly. I suppose I was rather keen on Batman, and used to roar about the house with some improvised cape pretending to be him. I'd be lying to say I remember the games I played, but the central attraction was definitely that Batman simply had the freedom to go and do whatever he wanted: a kind of Superman version of Bertie.

It's not hard with my own background to figure out why such a free spirit would be appealing. At some stage in our lives we've all dreamed of escaping some situation or environment. The fantasy option seems to take over when all logical options are closed off: Batman was my childish way of dealing with containment. I guess with most growing families that scene then converts to TV characters. It's just a more grown-up form through which kids can escape.

As I explained, TV didn't touch my life very much although I enjoyed the *Danger Man* and *Avengers* kind of adventure – which did get shown at acceptable times.

Because I was already so intensely focused on my playing, it was inevitable some of those around me would command admiration. The teacher Peter Norris was one in particular, as was Menuhin himself. As I try to explain in this book I actually wanted to play like the man. It's easy to imagine the wealth of knowledge he had to offer students, and his deep sense of the great European musical tradition was so infectious it survived in me and enhanced the years of American jazz influence. Indeed, it helped me integrate my involvement with that musical circle with my musical life as a whole.

Yehudi Menuhin obviously gets numerous mentions – simply because he has been part of my life since six years of age. It's a measure of the man that by the time he was of school-leaving age he'd played with great musicians such as Bartók, Busch, Ravel, Beecham and Elgar. He was actually born in New York but then lived in California; under the eagle eye of Louis Persinger, San Francisco Symphony's concertmaster, Menuhin developed his playing skills until, with Persinger accompanying him, he made his concert debut in Oakland playing Bériot's 'Scène de Ballet' – he was just seven! By the age of nine he'd made his New York recital debut, from where he went on to make his European premiere at eleven in Paris. It was there he met Georges Enesco, who was to become an important teaching influence on Menuhin. Writing, indeed reading, such dry statistics is so easy, yet to comprehend what is meant is much harder. Think of a friend who's got an eleven-year-old kid, recall the toys and videos he/she is into, and then imagine them standing on a huge stage in New York facing the best that Manhattan can muster as an audience. Then place the entire New York Symphony Orchestra just behind them, and expect a breathtaking performance of Beethoven from the little brat. That's exactly what Menuhin did in November of 1927 and, needless to say, garlanded himself in critical glory. He had a natural touch, a sensitivity and maturity which brought his playing to life and more and more flocked to watch this unique musician. By the time he was twenty, Menuhin had already enjoyed a world tour taking in thirteen separate countries. His professional career and commitment to pass on to others what he's learnt is brilliant. However, for me he was not in the proper sense a hero.

As I've just mentioned, Stephane Grappelli probably comes the closest. There was some sense of mystique around him; I was very conscious of its effect on me. He wasn't a pin-up, but I envied him the professional position he had carved out for himself – the feeling that he was his own man, enjoying his private life to the full, then stepping on stage to create his unique brand of jazz. He too was classically trained – at the Paris Conservatoire and, in turn, he looked up to the great jazz trumpeter Louis Armstrong. In fact, as a teenager he played in a big band styled on Jack Hylton's as well as summer seasons – even in the cinema, performing to silent movies. It was actually the breathtaking guitarist Django Reinhardt who formed a quintet with him and won the hearts of the Parisians. He stayed in Britain during the last war and when he met and played with Django again in 1946, the excitement between them had gone. He continued to develop his own thing over the years – always making his style even more distinctive. He and Menuhin actually made an album together – his natural instinct, just like the Impressionists', always lying back there just beneath the surface, ensuring the quality and structure of his work.

It's hardly a surprise that fiddlers feature strongly among my heroes, and my all-time favourites would be:

IVRY GITLIS: This guy is the most natural, original talent I have heard on record. The three records I have heard are his Bartók concerto, the Franck amd Debussy sonatas (with Martha Argerich), and the Tchaikovsky concerto. What is so remarkable about Gitlis is that if there is something exciting to communicate, he is not inhibited by the average critic's or violinist's preconception of what sound to use. With Gitlis you don't get that bland glossy sound expected and accepted from the 'leading' violinists today. Go for it, Ivry.

STEPHANE GRAPPELLI: Stephane's joie de vivre is apparent from every note he plays on the violin. After meeting the great violinist Eddie South, who guested on records with the Hot Club de Paris (the group Steff had with guitarist Django Reinhardt), Stephane himself became a major influence and encouragement to thousands of fiddlers wanting to use their instruments in jazz. I have described elsewhere in this book the liberating effect Steff had on my musical life.

SUGARCANE HARRIS: His work with Frank Zappa brought him to broad public attention. His solo on the 'Gumbo Variations' (on the *Hot Rats* album) is probably my favourite violin solo. It has a total blues feel and soul just pours out of the fiddle. It even survives a sacrilegious remix Zappa did for the CD reissue, where Zappa turns his own accompanimental guitar up and Sugarcane's violin down. I haven't heard much about him lately, but I really want to meet this guy and have a blow.

FRITZ KREISLER: Kreisler became one of my favourite players when I was in my early teens. What I was attracted to (apart from his brilliant compositions) was the spontaneity in his playing and his truly golden sound – probably the most beautiful ever to have come from a violin. His compositions, mainly composed on a short scale, helped to popularise him and the violin in a way few have ever achieved. His recordings of Beethoven concertos and with Rachmaninov are testament to his consummate musicianship, but the popular nature of his career drew disparaging remarks about his playing which proliferated far more than anything I've had to experience – which all helps me realise that if some clever guy puts some syllables in the right order at the expense of my playing (because of the popularity of my career) it's nothing to take too seriously! In fact, being in my position today, I can draw a lot from the inspiration given by old Fritz. On a personal note, after becoming interested in Kreisler, I found out that my grandfather played often with him and that, with William Primrose and Thomas Petrie, they actually made a record of Kreisler's own string quartet.

CHO LIANG LIN: When I went to the Juilliard School in New York, I suddenly found myself surrounded by the Dorothy DeLay stable. The amount of talent among her students was like if I'd been a young boxer, walking into the famous Kronk gym in Detroit. It was very exciting – among my contemporaries were Shlomo Mintz, Nadja Salerno-Sonnenberg, Joseph Swensen, Mark Piskanov, Mark Kaplan and Christian Altenberger. It was exciting to hear these players play at close quarters, but I remember the one who really stood out as a musician was Cho Liang Lin. When I heard him for the first time he was playing the Mendelssohn concerto (don't ask which one!) to about ten of us and we were listening to a master. He played the piece with aristocracy, impeccable taste, and total involvement and commitment. Needless to say, it was technically perfect as well. This was no whiz-kid showing what he could do – this was a real musician. The proof that he was no flash in the pan comes in the pudding! Jimmy's respect, responsibility and appetite for his art has become ever stronger over the years. Also, I have to add that Jimmy's recordings of Mozart are the only ones by any of my contemporaries that might persuade me that I'm wrong about the concertos!

YEHUDI MENUHIN: First of all, I might not have been a classical musician if it hadn't been for Yehudi's help when I was a kid. Apart from my particular debt to him, Yehudi is probably one of the most unique musicians of the century. He was playing better than any adult when he should have been having his nappies changed! And from the age of twelve to thirty he left us with recordings which haven't been bettered by anyone before or since. There are literally thousands of brats who can stun us with the speed of their fingers, but Yehudi has a gift given to one in a million fiddlers: the ability to convey the depth, nobility or poignancy of a simple melody.

GINETTE NEVUE: Her recordings of the 'Poème' by Chausson and the Sibelius concerto are possibly the finest around. Her playing is a wonderful mixture of the accuracy and firm tone control of Heifetz, and the serious musical phrasing of a player like Pablo Casals. Apart from the recording by Dmitry Sitkovetsky, I don't think there has been a musically valuable interpretation of the great Bach solo sonatas made in the last twenty-five years. Nevue's playing would have been perfect for those masterpieces but, unfortunately, we were deprived of such a contribution because, while still in the early stages of her career, she died in a plane crash.

MARK O'CONNOR: The Heifetz of the American folk world: at twelve Mark O'Connor was winning all the adult American country fiddle competitions. But he's not a hot whiz-kid. Nobody can play a melody more soulfully than Mark and every note he plays is a jewel. In addition, he has a humble spirit and doesn't give bullshit.

JEAN-LUC PONTY: Hearing Jean Luc Ponty's playing for the first time was a revelation. It was great to hear someone who could improvise structural solos at the same as really kicking ass. Some of my favourite work of his is the stuff he did with Frank Zappa, George Duke, and in particular an album called *Violin Summit* when, as a teenager, he rips into 'It Don't Mean A Thing', annihilating Stuff Smith, Stephane Grappelli and Sven Asmussen, who had soloed before him, and waking up a previously inanimate audience.

ALBERT SAMMONS: If Albert Sammons had been called Albert Sommonovich, he would be remembered alongside Kreisler, Szigeti and others as one of the greatest violinists of all time. As it was, he was born in a time when English violinists weren't meant to have an international career in classical music. Whereas many violinists get by with just one attribute and are called 'great', Sammons had two obvious great qualities: he had a beautiful tone quality, comparable to his pre-war contemporaries, Kreisler and Thibaud, and also had in his interpretations a structural understanding (intellectual and instinctive) not equalled until the arrival of Isaac Stern. He made possibly the greatest recordings of Elgar and Bruch concertos, and did this despite only having twelve fiddle lessons!

ISAAC STERN: Being at the Menuhin School, we used to get quite a bit of 'Menuhin does this, Menuhin does that' from the assistant violin teachers. So it was particularly exciting when a school friend of mine, David Angel, introduced me to the recordings of Isaac Stern. It was obvious on the first hearing that I was listening to one of the most important violinists ever born and he was approaching everything totally differently to Menuhin. Stern's main characteristics are his understanding and involvement in the architecture of a work, and his ability to communicate directly without over-complication (a feature he shares in common with Miles Davis). Stern is the opposite to most fiddle players, who only appreciate a melody and simply bask in the glory of their own sound.

There have been two occasions when I have looked up to players, admired them, wanted to meet them – only to be hugely disappointed. Sadly the disillusionment chiefly stemmed from attitudes born of a sense of self-importance, of cultural superiority because of foreign ancestry. I don't think about where someone comes from at all – providing we can understand each other and can play, that's all that counts. Religious or cultural snobbery just isn't in my vocabulary. To give you some idea about how little it concerns me, it was many years before it was explained to me that Jesus wasn't British. The disappointment when you meet someone famous who's not quite as tall/nice/talented as you'd expected is real. You always hope people are going to be as they seem, and yet so rarely is that really the case in any walk of life. Not too many people could feel that way about me. Simply being myself, whether likeable or not, pretty much ensures I'm the same most of the time.

It's odd really, because here I am, discussing an absence of any real pedigree in heroes and yet the mail bag brings quite a lot of letters declaring they are fans of mine! I just feel I have a job to do and it's part of my responsibility to ensure I'm always getting better, so I honestly don't feel that special. Sure, after gigs it's a bit of a crush and shopping is more eventful than it used to be. The thing is that most of the people come up and talk now, whereas a couple of years ago I'd probably have started off the chat. Being in music means you never ever actually get it all right: always you are striving for something more from these great compositions or from yourself. I hope that if anything of what I'm trying to do is attractive to youngsters, then it will be my independence: that what I've been able to do shows you *can* nurture your own expressions. Whatever talents you have locked away inside – they are very precious and 100 per cent you. Learn whatever you can from those you admire, and especially from those engaged in coaching you. Much of it may feel pretty redundant, but later on a fair bit of it will become vital background knowledge. In order to be as inventive and exciting as a Stephane Grappelli, you have to know all your basic stuff first.

This century has seen a lot of change. In the '30s and '40s jazz took over from classical as being the most socially relevant music, then in the '50s rock music related to people's lives in a more meaningful way and so replaced jazz. Now jazz and classical and many other kinds of music are reaching levels of popularity and social consciousness equal to that previously held only by rock music. It's a time when musicians and audiences alike are realising that good music isn't too good for most people, it's actually too good *not* to be listened to by most people . . . Whatever some 'experts' might say, let's get on with it!

Recordings

Recordings

Nigel Kennedy Plays Jazz
with Peter Pettinger, Piano

1 Body and Soul
2 Bag's Groove
3 Autumn Leaves
4 Swing '39
5 Isn't She Lovely
6 Lover Man
7 The Girl from Ipanema

Produced by Brian Couzens
Chandos Records Limited, 1984
(formerly released as *Strad Jazz*)

'*Strad Jazz* (Kennedy's own title idea as he plays a Stradivarius violin) includes a variety of numbers including "The Girl from Ipanema", "Autumn Leaves", "Isn't She Lovely" and "Body and Soul". It also includes "Swing '39", a number originally written by Django Reinhardt and Stephane Grappelli – appropriate, because it was the ageless French violinist who first introduced Kennedy to jazz violin when he was a stripling at the Menuhin School.'

(*Music Week*)

Edward Elgar Sonata for Violin and Piano

Produced by Brian Couzens
Sound Engineer – Brian Couzens
Chandos Records Limited, 1985

Let Loose

1 Let Loose
2 Zigane
3 Emotion
4 The Way It Is
5 The Way We Were
6 Killer Instinct
7 Impro 1
8 Drive
9 Way Outside

Recorded and mixed at Elephant Studios, London, April 1987
Co-produced by Nigel Kennedy and Nick Robbins
Engineered by Nick Robbins
Drum programmes by Dave Heath
All arrangements by Nigel Kennedy and Dave Heath except 'Drive' arranged by Dominic Miller and Nigel Kennedy
EMI Records Limited, 1987

'In an age of rampant specialisation, one draws some encouragement from Nigel Kennedy's refusal to be tied to any one kind of repertoire. "When I play the violin I try to get away from the virtuoso stereotype associated with the instrument," he says. He couldn't get much further away from the "virtuoso stereotype" than this. Designated a "rock-jazz" album, *Let Loose* aims directly at the popular market, though Kennedy, being the musician he is, obviously feels the need for greater contrast than the format of a rock album usually admits.'

(*Gramophone*)

Elgar Violin Concerto in B minor, Op. 61
London Philharmonic Orchestra
Conducted by Vernon Handley

1 I Allegro
2 II Andante
3 III Allegro molto – Cadenza – Allegro molto

Produced by Andrew Keener
Recording Engineer: Mike Clements
Gramophone Award – Record of the Year, 1985
Best Classical Disc – BPI, 1986
BPI Silver Disc Award
BPI Gold Disc Award
EMI Records Limited, 1984

'I've never heard a cleaner, more vital or impassioned performance of the piece.

Kennedy's live-wire playing and pinpont intonation come extremely close to the Heifetz sound. They reach out and grab you by the throat. But in addition to that, Kennedy also offers a bit more expansive phrasing and smouldering Romantic warmth – à la Menuhin at his best. In some way, he tops even Itzhak Perlman in both departments. Then, too, Kennedy throws himself into the passage work with cheek and daring as well as maturity.

Best of all, with wonderful orchestral support, Kennedy reaches the dark hints of tragedy in this masterpiece with almost Mahlerian fervour. The result is an awesome performance, made all the more freaky by the fact that it's a debut disc. One looks forward to more Kennedy recordings – especially if they will let him have a crack at the Walton Concerto! Highest recommendation.'

(*San Francisco Chronicle*)

Music by Ellington & Bartók

Bartók: Sonata for Solo Violin
1 1st Movement: Tempo di ciaccona
2 2nd Movement: Fuga – Risoluto, non troppo vivo
3 3rd Movement: Melodia – Adagio
4 4th Movement: Presto

Duke Ellington: Mainly Black
5 Introduction
6 Come Sunday
7 Work Song

8 The Blues (Mauve)
9 Come Sunday

with Alec Dankworth, double bass

Recorded in No. 1 Studio, Abbey Road, London, 1986
Produced by Andrew Keener
Balance Engineer: Mike Clements
EMI Records Limited, 1986

'Nigel Kennedy's account is the most warmly lyrical that I have heard, his tone beautiful and expressive in even the most hair-raising passages. The notorious hazards are expertly negotiated, but in this reading one is more likely to notice subtler manifestations of virtuosity: the clarity and character of the part-writing in the fugue or the exquisite range of colour and dynamic shading in the slow movement.'

(*Gramophone*)

Tchaikovsky Violin Concerto in D major, Op. 35
London Philharmonic Orchestra
Conducted by Okko Kamu

1 1st Movement – Allegro moderato
2 2nd Movement – Canzonetta, andante
3 3rd Movement – Finale, allegro vivacissimo

Chausson Poème for Violin and Orchestra, Op. 25
1 Poème Op. 25

Recorded at Walthamstow Assembly Hall, 1985
Produced by Andrew Keener
Balance Engineer: Mike Clements
EMI Records Limited, 1986

'This is the most distinctive recording of Tchaikovsky's Violin Concerto I have heard for a decade or more, and if Kennedy had not won the *Gramophone* Award for Elgar's Concerto a couple of years ago, he could have expected to win it with this. The imagination and care that has gone into the presentation of every phase of this immensely popular work cannot be overlooked or forgotten yet a feeling of total spontaneity pervades the recording. In that sense, it almost sounds like a concert performance.'

(*Music Week*)

Walton Violin and Viola Concertos
Royal Philharmonic Orchestra
Conducted by André Previn

Viola Concerto
1 | Andante comodo
2 || Vivo, con molto preciso
3 ||| Allegro moderato

Violin Concerto
4 | Andante tranquillo
5 || Presto capriccioso alla Napolitana – Trio (canzonetta) – Tempo I
6 ||| Vivace

Recorded in No. 1 Studio, Abbey Road, London, 1987
Produced by Andrew Keener
Balance engineer: Mark Vigars
EMI Records Limited, 1987

'I shall be surprised if the new version of the first two of them [concertos], by Nigel Kennedy with the Royal Philharmonic Orchestra under André Previn, does not establish itself as a long-lasting classic ... This young player has quickly become a national asset; and his 1985 award-winning version of Elgar's Violin Concerto (also on EMI) with the LPO under Vernon Handley is deservedly famous. Now comes his Walton coupling, which has every chance of repeating that notable success, and every claim to do so.'

(*Sunday Times*)

Mendelssohn and Bruch Violin Concertos
English Chamber Orchestra
Conducted by Jeffrey Tate

Bruch: Violin Concerto No. 1 in G minor, Op. 26
1 | Vorspiel (Allegro moderato)
2 || Adagio
3 ||| Finale (Allegro energico)
4 Schubert: Rondo in A for violin and strings

Mendelssohn: Violin Concerto in E minor, Op. 64
5 | Allegro molto appassionato
6 || Andante
7 ||| Allegretto non troppo – Allegro molto vivace

Recorded in No. 1 Studio, Abbey Road, London, 1987
Produced by Andrew Keener
Balance Engineer: Mark Vigars
BPI Silver Disc Award
BPI Gold Disc Award
EMI Records Limited, 1988

'Kennedy has shrewdly augmented the regular concerto coupling of Bruch and Mendelssohn with the rare Schubert work, and the result is a generous issue which on every front can be warmly recommended for exceptionally strong and positive performances, vividly recorded.

... When it comes to the two main works, Kennedy readily holds his own against all comers. His view of the Mendelssohn has a positive, masculine quality established at the very start.

... The Bruch brings another warm and positive performance, consistently sympathetic, with the orchestra once more adding to the power. Kennedy is more than a match for the rival versions I have listed, again bringing a masculine strength which goes with a richly expressive yet totally unsentimental view of Bruch's exuberant lyricism, as in the central slow movement. Plainly nowadays Kennedy enjoys himself in the studio more than ever.'

(*Gramophone*)

Sibelius Violin Concerto and Symphony No. 5
City of Birmingham Symphony Orchestra
Conducted by Simon Rattle

Violin Concerto in D minor, Op. 47
1 | Allegro moderato
2 || Adagio di molto
3 ||| Allegro, ma non tanto

Symphony No. 5 in E flat, Op. 82*
4 | Tempo molto moderato – Allegro moderato
5 || Andante mosso, quasi allegretto
6 ||| Allegro molto – Un pochettino largamente

Recorded at the Arts Centre, University of Warwick, 1987
Produced by Andrew Kenner (*and David R. Murray)
Balance Engineer: Michael Sheady
EMI Records Limited, 1988

'... [This] work which on record, harnessed with other display pieces, has generally been treated as a virtuoso vehicle rather than a Sibelius piece.

With Rattle's taut and powerful orchestral control added to Kennedy's expressive warmth, extrovert but concentrated, it makes a richly satisfying reading, ending with a spectacular account of the finale at high speed.'

(*Guardian*)

Vivaldi: The Four Seasons (Le quattro stagioni)
English Chamber Orchestra (directed by Nigel Kennedy)

Concerto No. 1 in E 'La primavera'
1 | Allegro
2 || Largo
3 ||| Allegro

Concerto No. 2 in G minor 'L'estate'
4 | Allegro non molto

5 || Adagio
6 ||| Presto

Concerto No. 3 in F 'L'autunno'
7 | Allegro
8 || Adagio molto
9 ||| Allegro

Concerto No. 4 in F minor 'L'inverno'
10 | Allegro non molto
11 || Largo
12 ||| Allegro

Recorded in the Church of St John-at-Hackney, London 1986 and 1989
Produced by Andrew Keener
Balance Engineers: Mike Clements and Mike Hatch
Classical Chart Entry at No. 1
BPI Silver Disc Award
BPI Gold Disc Award
BPI Double Gold Disc Award
BPI Platinum Disc Award
BPI Double Platinum Disc Award
EMI Records Limited, 1989

'He really goes for it, all the time, in a generally fast set of performances that are full of attack, bubbling with new ideas and which generally blow the cobwebs out of even the most familiar corners of the *Four Seasons*.'

(*Guardian*)

Also available on Video: 'Golden Rose of Montreux' Award Winner
Vivaldi Four Seasons
Nigel Kennedy and the English Chamber Orchestra
Recorded at Westway Studios, London, 1990
Directed by Geoff Wonfor
Producers: Andrea Wonfor and Chips Chipperfield
Editor: Andy Matthews

A Picture Music International Release
EMI Records Limited, 1990

Brahms Violin Concerto in D, Op. 77
The London Philharmonic
Conducted by Klaus Tennstedt

1 | Allegro non troppo
2 || Adagio
3 ||| Allegro giocoso, ma non troppo vivace

Recorded in No. 1 Studio, Abbey Road, London, 1990
Producer and Editor: Andrew Keener
Balance Engineer: Mike Clements (Floating Earth)
BPI Silver Disc Award
BPI Gold Disc Award
EMI Records Limited, 1991

'My surprise was to find, when comparing this exaggerated reading with some of my favourites from the past, Grumiaux, Perlman, Menuhin with Furtwängler, not to mention an excellent new contender from ASV, the Chinese Xue-Wei, Kennedy more than held his own. Exaggerated it may be, but this is a performance with real heart and individuality. It conveys not only intense concentration over long spans (thanks in good measure to Klaus Tennstedt's masterly accompaniment with the LPO), but genuine spontaneity in the phrasing and rhythmic pointing, to make you sit up and listen afresh at unexpected details.'

(*Guardian*)

Also available on Video:
Brahms Violin Concerto
The London Philharmonic
Conducted by Klaus Tennstedt

Recorded at Westway Studios, London, 1991

Directed by Geoff Wonfor
Producer: Chips Chipperfield
Editor: Andy Matthews
A Picture Music International Release
EMI Records Limited, 1991